Theories of
Communication

Theories of Communication

A Short Introduction

Armand Mattelart and Michèle Mattelart

Translated by Susan Gruenheck Taponier
and James A. Cohen

SAGE Publications
London • Thousand Oaks • New Delhi

Originally published as *Histoire des théories de la
communication* © Éditions La Découverte, Paris, 1995

Translation © Susan Gruenheck Taponier
and James A. Cohen 1998
First published in English 1998

Reprinted 2004

This translation has been published with financial support
from the Ministère Français de la Culture

All rights reserved. No part of this publication may be
reproduced, stored in a retrieval system, transmitted or
utilized in any form or by any means, electronic, mechanical,
photocopying, recording or otherwise, without permission
in writing from the Publishers.

 SAGE Publications Ltd
6 Bonhill Street
London EC2A 4PU

SAGE Publications Inc
2455 Teller Road
Thousand Oaks, California 91320

SAGE Publications India Pvt Ltd
32, M-Block Market
Great Kailash – I
New Delhi 110 048

British Library Cataloguing in Publication data

A catalogue record for this book is
available from the British Library

ISBN 0 7619 5646 8
ISBN 0 7619 5647 6 (pbk)

Library of Congress catalog record available

Typeset by M Rules

Contents

Introduction

The notion of communication covers a multitude of meanings. While this has long been the case, the proliferation of technologies and the professionalisation of practices have added further voices to the late twentieth-century polyphony that has turned communication into the very symbol of society in the third millennium.

Situated at the crossroads of several disciplines, communication processes have aroused the interest of sciences as diverse as philosophy, history, geography, psychology, sociology, ethnology, economics, political science, biology, cybernetics and the cognitive sciences. Moreover, in the course of its development, this particular field of social science has been continually obsessed by the question of its own scientific legitimacy. This has led it to borrow scientific models from the natural sciences and adapt them by analogy.

The present work is an attempt to account for the multiplicity and diversity of this field of scientific observation, historically caught in the tension between material and immaterial networks, biological and social paradigms, nature and culture, technical devices and speech, economics and culture, micro and macro perspectives, village and globe, actor and system, free will and social determinisms. The history of theories of communication is a record of these tensions and of the varied attempts to articulate – or avoid articulating – the terms of what all too often have appeared as dichotomies and binary oppositions rather than levels of analysis. In diverse historical contexts and formulated in various ways, these tensions and antagonisms have constantly manifested themselves, dividing the field into different schools of thought, currents and tendencies.

These lasting tensions invalidate any strictly chronological approach to the history of theories. The ebb and flow of the approaches precludes a linear conception of theoretical development. While this book roughly follows a chronological order in presenting these schools, currents and trends, it emphasises the circularity of approaches. Old debates over objects and research strategies considered long since resolved or dated suddenly reappear, calling into question modes of intelligibility and 'regimes of truth' that have held sway for decades. One of the most striking illustrations of this phenomenon was the return of the ethnographic approach in the 1980s, in the context of a crisis in totalising views of society.

The notion of communication theory poses just as many problems as that of communication itself and it, too, has given rise to contradictory debate. First, as often happens in the human and social sciences, there is strong opposition between one school or epistemology and another concerning the status and definition of the theory. Moreover, the term 'school' may be misleading. Indeed, a school may well harbour a number of different currents and be far from possessing the uniformity its name would suggest. Finally, discourse on communication is often promoted to the ranks of general theory without proper assessment. The clever formulae of Marshall McLuhan stand side by side with the weighty philosophical constructions of Jürgen Habermas, and we are at a loss to say which of the two has more radically changed our way of looking at the technological environment.

Certain doctrines, with their trendy, ready-made thinking and meteoric neologisms, claim to be definitive explanatory systems, authoritative lessons, erasing in their wake slowly accumulated, contradictory, interdisciplinary discoveries and learning, thereby reinforcing the impression that their object of study is frivolous. In this field of knowledge, perhaps more than in any other, there is a widely held illusion that we can reduce accumulated knowledge to a *tabula rasa* and that, unlike in other disciplines, everything has yet to be created.

1 *The Social Organism*

The nineteenth century, during which the basic technical systems of communication and the principle of free trade were invented, saw the introduction of notions supporting a vision of communication as an integrating factor of human societies. The notion of communication originally centred on the question of physical networks and was a central element of the ideology of progress. By the end of the century, it came to encompass the management of multitudes of human beings. The idea of society as an organism, that is, a whole composed of organs performing pre-determined functions, inspired the earliest conceptions of a 'science of communication'.

1 The discovery of trade and flows

The division of labour

The 'division of labour', initially formulated in scientific terms in the eighteenth century by Adam Smith (1723–90), represented the first theoretical step. Communication contributed to organising collective labour within factories and structuring economic activity. In the commercial *cosmopolis* of the laissez-faire system, the division of labour and the channels of communication (river, maritime and overland routes) were synonymous with opulence and growth. England had already achieved its 'circulation revolution' which was starting to be incorporated quite naturally into the new landscape of the industrial revolution then in progress.

In contrast, during the same period, France was still attempting to unify its internal market. In this agrarian monarchy, discourse on the virtues of communication systems was directly proportionate to their deficiency. For a long time, the French vision of communication as a vector of progress and the fulfilment of reason was characterised by the gap between reality and a voluntaristic theory on how to domesticate movement. This was first expressed by François Quesnay (1694–1774) and the school of the Physiocrats, inventors of the maxim 'Laissez faire, laissez passer', which was taken up by economic liberalism in the second half of the nineteenth century. Faithful to the Enlightenment postulate according to which trade generates a creative power, they proclaimed the necessity for the enlightened despot of agrarian France to liberalise the flow of goods and manpower and support a policy of building and maintaining communication routes, offering China as an example.

Quesnay studied economic circuits as a whole, attempting to grasp them as 'systems' or 'units'. A doctor by profession, he drew inspiration from his knowledge of the two-way circulation of blood, and developed a diagram representing the circulation of wealth in a *Tableau économique* (*Economic chart*) (1758). The chart offers a macroscopic vision of an economy of 'flows' in the form of a geometrical zigzag figure in which the lines expressing exchange between human beings and the land, as well as among the three classes making up society, cut across each other and become intertwined. The revolutionary process of 1789 released these flows by taking measures, such as adopting the metric system, that were intended to speed up the unification of the national territory. Claude Chappe's optical telegraph, the first remote communications system, was inaugurated in 1793. It was invented for military purposes. The notion of the division of labour and the model of material flows provided sustenance to the school of English classical economics, and, in particular, the analyses of John Stuart Mill (1806–73), prefiguring 'a cybernetic model of material flows with feedback flows of money *qua* information' (Beniger, 1992). The concept of the division of labour also stimulated the reflections of Charles Babbage (1792–1871) on the 'division of mental labour' and led him to draw up projects for mechanising intellectual operations, the 'difference engine' and the 'analytical engine' or 'number mill', ancestors of the huge electronic calculators that preceded the invention of the computer.

Networks and the organic totality

Another key concept is that of network. Claude Henri de Saint-Simon (1760–1825) renewed the interpretation of the social using the metaphor of the living being. This marked the advent of the organism as network (Musso, 1990). Saint-Simon's 'social physiology' presented itself as a science of social reorganisation, allowing for the transition from 'governing human beings' to 'administering things'. In this model, society was conceived as an organic system, a bundle or fabric of networks, but also as an 'industrial system' managed by and as an industry. In association with the ideas of the public works engineers of his time, Saint-Simon attributed strategic importance to the development of a system of communication routes and the establishment of a credit system. In his view, the circulation of money, like that of blood for the human heart, brought unified life to society conceived as one vast industry.

From this philosophy of industrialism, his disciples retained an operative idea to hasten the advent of what they called the 'positive age': the organising function at work in the production of artificial networks, those of both transport–communication ('material networks') and finance ('spiritual networks'). They created railway lines, bank companies, interoceanic canals (Suez and Panama) and shipping companies and took charge of the great universal exhibitions.

Saint-Simonism symbolised the spirit of enterprise of the second half of the nineteenth century. In the mentality of the age, his philosophy of progress influenced not only Eugène Sue's serial novels and their ideas for peacefully reconciling social antagonisms but also Jules Verne's science fiction stories about technical worlds.

In the same half-century, Herbert Spencer (1820–1903), a railway engineer turned philosopher, took the idea of communication as an organic system even further. His 'social physiology' – which existed in outline form in 1852, seven years before the publication of Darwin's major work, *The Origin of Species*, and was explicitly formulated starting in 1870 – carried to an extreme the hypothesis of continuity between the biological and the social order. The physiological division of labour and the progress of the organism went together. From the homogeneous to the heterogeneous, from the simple to the complex, from concentration to differentiation, industrial society is the embodiment of 'organic society': an increasingly coherent, integrated society-as-organism in which functions are increasingly well defined and parts increasingly interdependent. In this systematic whole, communication is a basic component of organic systems of distribution and regulation. Like the vascular system, the former (made up of roads, canals and railways) ensures the distribution of nutritive substance. The latter functions as the equivalent to the nervous system, making it possible to manage the complex relations between a dominant centre and its periphery. This is the role of information (the press, petitions, surveys) and of all the means of communication by which the centre can 'propagate its influence', such as the postal service, the telegraph and news agencies. Dispatches are compared to nervous discharges that communicate movement from an inhabitant of one city to that of another.

History as development

Another fundamental notion of communication systems analysis is that of development. Spencer created the English version of positivist sociology. A few decades earlier, Auguste Comte (1798–1857), a former disciple of Saint-Simon, had formulated the basic tenets of a positive science of human societies in his *Cours de philosophie positive*, written between 1830 and 1842, without paying special attention to organs or communication systems. Unlike Spencer, who combined biology and the physics of energy and force, Comte limited himself to biology, even though he dubbed his sociological project a 'social physics' and saw it as the 'genuine science of social development'. He combined the concept of division of labour with the notions of development, growth, the process of perfection, homogeneity, differentiation and heterogeneity – notions which he had borrowed directly from embryology. For Comte, as for Spencer, society as a collective organism obeyed the physiological law of progressive development.

History was conceived as the succession of three 'stages' or 'eras': the theological or fictional stage, the metaphysical or abstract stage and finally the positive or scientific stage. The third was synonymous with industrial society, the age of reality, utility, organisation and science and the decline of all non-scientific forms of knowledge, even if all the disciplines were far from having attained synchronous development.

Comte's biographical conception of history as necessity, divided into stages, without detours, reversals or regressions and guided by the notion of linear progress, was similar to that developed in the second half of the nineteenth century in ethnology and political economy. Social Darwinism transposed this order of chronological succession on to the moral order and even the order of 'races'. This division into periods was frequently used to justify designating certain peoples as 'primitive' or 'child-like' and thus keeping them under colonial domination until they 'matured' into 'adults'. This process of maturing was seen as a passage through certain stages already crossed by the so-called 'civilised' nations – a stage considered indispensable for successful evolution.

Out of this representation of human societal development as 'history in fragments', in the words of historian Fernand Braudel, came the first formulations of diffusionist theory according to which progress can only reach the periphery through the radiation of values outwards from the centre. These theories were put to the test by the violent contact between cultures in the age of empires (1875–1914) and their main proponents were ethnologists and geographers. They were to be revitalised after World War II by the sociology of modernisation and its conception of 'development' in which the media were attributed a strategic role (see Chapter 2.2).

By the end of the nineteenth century, the biological model of social life had become the common-sense way of describing communication systems as developing and civilising agents (A. Mattelart, 1994).

In 1897, the German theorist Friedrich Ratzel (1844–1904) laid the foundations for political geography or geopolitics, the science of geographical space and its control. According to Ratzel, 'The state is an organism rooted in the soil' and the purpose of this science was to study the organic relations maintained by the state with its territory. Networks and circuits, trade, interaction, mobility, are all expressions of vital energy; networks and circuits 'vitalise' the territory. In this reflection on the spatial dimension of power, space becomes 'vital space'.

2 Managing the multitudes

Moral statistics and the average man

What is the nature of the new society heralded by the rise of multitudes in the city? This question lay at the heart of the 'mass society' approach and its corollary, the study of the means of mass dissemination, which developed in the last two decades of the nineteenth century.

The masses were presented as a real or potential threat to society as a whole, and this danger justified setting up a system for statistical control of judicial and demographic flows (Desrosières, 1993).

Around 1835, the Belgian astronomer and mathematician Adolphe Quételet (1796–1874) founded a new science of social measurement which he called 'social physics'. The basic unit of this science was the 'average man', seen as equivalent to the body's centre of gravity, a starting point from which pathologies, crises and imbalances of the social order could be assessed. Quételet drew up not only tables of mortality, but also 'tables of criminality', from which he attempted to derive an index of the 'penchant for crime' in correlation with sex, age, climate and social condition, in order to extract the laws of a moral order seen as parallel to the physical order.

Quételet may be credited for institutionalising probability theory. Foreshadowed by Pascal's 'geometry of chance', probability theory was an invitation to a new way of governing people: 'insurance society' (Ewald, 1986). The technology of risk and reasoning in terms of probability, already at work in managing private insurance applied to mortality, shipping risks and fires, was transferred to the political field and became a tool for managing individuals considered *en masse*. In the course of this shift from civil to social law, towards calculated solidarity and interdependence, there arose the principle of the welfare state that socialised responsibility and reduced all social problems to a question of odds. The notion of solidarity eluded the voluntaristic discourse of charity and fraternity and instead espoused the language of the necessary biological interdependence of living cells. It laid the foundations for the security of the individual, who could feel part of a whole, through a contractual relationship – and an indebtedness as well – beginning at birth. This notion of solidarity also became a basis for the interdependence of nations. The biomorphic notion of interdependence in turn provided the foundation for the idea of necessary communication.

Half a century after Quételet's project to calculate social pathologies, the criminal sciences involving human measurement arose. Nomenclatures and indexes were used by judges, the police and court doctors to codify and fulfil their mission of social hygiene through the surveillance and normalisation of the so-called dangerous classes. Bertillon's 'anthropometry', Galton's biometrics and eugenics and Lombroso's criminal anthropology all aimed to identify individuals and establish their 'profiles'.

Although the typology of readerships first appeared in media management with the creation of women's magazines in the United States in the 1880s and was perfected under the Fordist system in the 1920s, reasoning in terms of probability was not applied to rationalising mass communication until the 1930s (see Chapter 2.2).

The psychology of crowds

Discussions about the political nature of a public opinion newly freed from constraints on freedom of the press and assembly gave rise to the 'psychology of crowds'. This project was formulated by Italian sociologist Scipio Sighele (1868–1913) and by the French doctor of psychopathology Gustave Le Bon (1841–1931). Both subscribed to the same manipulative vision of society.

Sighele's essay, *La Folla criminale* (*The Criminal Crowd*), published in Turin in 1891 and translated into French the following year, extrapolated from individual psychology to 'collective psychology'. Under the concept of 'crimes of the crowd ', Sighele included every sort of 'collective plebeian violence', from labour strikes to popular uprisings. In every crowd, there are those who lead and those who are led, the hypnotists and the hypnotised. Only the 'power of suggestion' explains why the latter blindly follow the former. The new forms of suggestion represented by the press, hardly mentioned in the first edition of the book, were widely discussed in the second, published in 1901, in which journalists – especially those covering trials – were depicted as ringleaders while their readership was 'the wet plaster on which their hands leave an imprint'.

In Sighele's analysis, suggestion and hallucination – terms that indicate the influence of alienist Jean-Martin Charcot – transformed individuals caught up in a crowd into automatons or sleepwalkers. In very similar terms (to the point of being publicly accused of plagiarism by Sighele), Le Bon analysed the behaviour of multitudes in *Psychologie des foules* (*The Crowd: A Study in the Popular Mind*) (1895). Whereas the Italian sociologist included in his study of crowds the revolts of have-nots, Le Bon, who was opposed to egalitarian ideologies, condemned all forms of collective reasoning, which he interpreted as a regression in the evolution of human society. Before discussing the psychology of crowds, he theorised about the psychology of peoples, making the racial factor a decisive element in the hierarchy of civilisations. His argument concerning the 'soul of the crowd', which he saw as an autonomous being with respect to the individuals that compose it, is thus inseparable from his analyses of the 'soul of the race' and the impulsive, non-rational character of all 'inferior peoples' and their after-images in civilised societies, 'children and women'.

In answer to these authors, the magistrate Gabriel Tarde (1843–1904) retorted that the age of crowds was already a thing of the past and that society was entering the 'age of publics'. Contrary to the crowd, which was a concert of psychic contagion essentially produced by physical contact, the public (or publics), a product of the long history of the means of transport and dissemination, 'progresses along with sociability'. People can only belong to one crowd at a time, but they can be part of several publics at the same time, and this complexity requires examination of its effects on the evolution of groups (parties, parliaments and scientific, religious and professional groups). Unlike his predecessors, Tarde did not complain about the apocalyptic surge of the 'populace-crowd'.

Tarde continued to be heavily influenced by the notion of suggestion and suggestibility, and his notions of imitation and counter-imitation as a social bond were connected to it. Although he also discussed invention – the other motor of social relationships – his notion of imitation, derived from a social theory of great conceptual richness, was frequently deformed later on, taken out of context and retained as the sole determining factor in sociability.

In 1921, Sigmund Freud (1856–1939) disputed the two axioms of crowd psychology, namely that the mass exalts affectivity and inhibits thought. He criticised what he called the 'tyranny of suggestion' as a 'magical' explanation of the transformation of the individual. To clarify the 'essence of the soul of the crowd', he had recourse to the concept of libido which he had tested in the study of neuroses. If an individual abandons his singularity in the crowd and allows himself to be influenced by the suggestion of others, he does so 'because he feels the need of being in harmony with them rather than in opposition to them – so that perhaps after all he does it "*ihnen zu liebe*" (for their sake)' (Freud, 1921).

Tarde's social psychology was clearly opposed to the positive sociology of Émile Durkheim (1858–1917). Tarde reproached Durkheim for considering social phenomena separately from the conscious subjects that form representations of them and for treating them as external things. In seeking to account for the subjective nature of social interaction so as to avoid reifying social facts, Tarde's aim was in line with the project of Georg Simmel (1858–1918). As opposed to an organicist sociology inclined to see individual conduct only as a reaction to given conditions or to external 'social facts', Simmel saw social phenomena arising from exchanges, relations and reciprocal action between individuals, that is, an intersubjective movement or a 'network of affiliations'. Contrary to a sociology that defined its object as institutional or structural entities such as the state, the family, social classes, churches, corporate bodies and interest groups, Simmel was interested in the 'small objects' of everyday collective life. That is where he thought he could discern most clearly the twofold and paradoxical process that characterises social phenomena, composed of the complementary, concomitant relations of 'sociation' and 'dissociation'. The former, which he expressed by the metaphor of the bridge (*Brücke*), corresponds to the individual's ability to associate what has been taken separated or dissociated. The second, which he conveys in the metaphor of the door (*Tür*), is the individual's capacity to separate and thus accede to another order of meaning (Javeau, 1986; Quéré, 1988).

Until the 1980s, the Durkheimian tradition remained uncontested in French-speaking countries, overshadowing this other sociological tradition and its analysis of social relations as communicative interactions.

Technique and utopias

The end of the nineteenth century was a fertile period for utopian discourse and the imaginary of redeeming technologies. For the Russian anarchist geographer, Piotr Kropotkin, and the Scottish sociologist, Patrick Geddes, electrical networks, with their decentralising virtues, contained the promise of a new form of communal existence, reconciling labour and leisure, manual and intellectual labour and city and country life. The neo-technical age that followed the paleotechnical, mechanical and imperial age could only signify the advent of a horizontal, transparent society.

In *News from Nowhere* (1891), William Morris sketched out the stages of the future Communist society of plenty set in nature and rediscovered as a result of a revolution governed by reason. The first stage – that of socialism – would be characterised by the unprecedented development of machines, enabling humanity to enter the golden age of Communism. Morris postulated that only the transformation of the material basis of social life could open the way to the era of cultural change. To reach utopian society, Morris, who was a theoretician of art, poetry and painting and a founding member of the Socialist League, was ready to accept a temporary eclipse of art in order to recover it in a world released from capitalist oppression and corruption, in which art could return to the pure, natural sources of beauty. Machines would be available to spare this new mankind from any unpleasant, hard labour.

In a work published in 1888 entitled *Looking Backward (2000–1887)*, the New England socialist Edward Bellamy imagined a society in which major industries had been nationalised and radio – the 'collective telephone' whose invention he predicted – would be used to mobilise everyone into an 'industrial army' leading to a communal society of plenty.

In 1872, the liberal thinker Samuel Butler published a work opposed to this instrumental conception of technology seen as a source of social salvation. In *Erewhon*, an anagram of 'Nowhere', that is, utopia, Butler raised the problem of the slow metamorphosis of human subjectivity within the context of the rise of technical rationality.

2 New World Empiricism

As early as the first decade of the twentieth century, the theme of communication in the United States went hand in hand with the construction of the social sciences on an empirical foundation. The so-called Chicago School was the first centre of this movement. Its micro-sociological approach to the modes of communication used in community organisation was in harmony with the idea that the social sciences could play a role in solving great social problems. The supremacy of this school lasted until the just before World War II. In the 1940s, another current arose that specialised in what was called 'mass communication research'. Its functionalist schema of analysis oriented research towards quantitative studies adapted to the needs of media managers.

1 The Chicago School and human ecology

The city as a 'spectroscope of society'

One figure stands out among the members of the Chicago School: Robert Ezra Park (1864–1944). Author of a doctoral thesis prepared in Heidelberg on 'The Crowd and the Public' (1903), Park became a reporter and a supporter of civil rights for blacks. Even after joining the university in 1913, he continued practising journalism and considered the sociological surveys he carried out in urban areas as a higher form of reporting. He followed the teachings of Georg Simmel, who thought of the city as a 'state of mind' and saw the psychological basis of the 'urban personality' in 'intensification of nervous stimulation', 'mobility' and 'locomotion' (Simmel, 1903). Park was also among the first to introduce the work of Tarde to the United States. In contrast to the European speculative sociology of the time, the concepts that Tarde and Simmel brought to Americans were closer to 'concrete situations', and more helpful in forging the tools they needed to analyse 'attitudes' and 'behaviour'.

The field of investigation privileged by the Chicago School was the city as a 'social laboratory' with its symptoms of disorganisation, marginality, acculturation and assimilation, or the city as the locus of 'mobility'. Between 1915 and 1935, the most important contributions of its scholars were devoted to immigration and the question of how immigrants become integrated into US society. Starting from ethnic communities, Park reflected on the assimilating function of newspapers (especially the innumerable foreign-language publications), the nature of information, professional journalism and what distinguishes it from 'social propaganda' or municipal advertising (Park, 1922).

In 1921, Park and his colleague E.W. Burgess founded a discipline they called 'human ecology'. The term referred to a concept invented in 1859 by Ernest Haeckel, a German biologist, who defined ecology as the science of the relationship between the organism and the environment, understood in the broadest sense as the sum total of the conditions of existence. Quoting extensively from the work of botanists and zoologists as well as that of Spencer,

Park and Burgess presented their programme as a systematic attempt to apply the theoretical framework of plant and animal ecology to the study of human communities.

A community was defined by three elements: a population that is territorially organised, more or less completely rooted in its territory, and whose individual units live in a relationship of mutual interdependence that is symbiotic rather than societal. In this 'biological economics', a term that Park sometimes used as a synonym for human ecology, relationships between individuals are governed by the 'struggle for space'. Competition functions as an organising principle. In human society, competition and the division of labour result in forms of unplanned competitive cooperation that make up the symbiotic relations or the 'biotic' level of human organisation. This 'sub-social level' is the expression of the web of life, 'binding living creatures all over the world into a vital nexus'. This 'organic community', whose population is scattered from both a territorial and a functional standpoint as soon as it enters into competition, can be óbserved in its various phases or successive periods (Park, 1936). Park used this schema to account for the 'cycle of ethnic relations' (competition, conflict, adaptation, assimilation) in immigrant communities.

Park posited a theoretical opposition between 'biotic substructure' and the social or cultural level, which is conceived as a superstructure erected on top of it, and which functions as a necessary 'instrument of direction and control'. This level is managed by the community as well as by the consensus (or moral order) which regulates competition, thereby giving individuals the opportunity to share an experience and establish ties to society. Culture is at once a body of customs and beliefs and a set of artefacts and tools or technological systems. This level does not fall directly within the province of the new ecological science.

According to human ecology, any change affecting the existing division of labour or the relations of the population to the land is conceived in terms of equilibrium, crisis and a return to equilibrium: 'It investigates the processes by which the "biotic balance" and "social equilibrium" are maintained once they are achieved and the processes by which, when the biotic balance and the social equilibrium are disturbed, the transition is made from one relatively stable order to another' (Park, 1936).

The original dichotomy between biotic and social levels created by human ecology gave rise to much discussion in the period between the wars. Many scholars accused Park of severing the competitive process from the socio-cultural matrix that defined its rules and of succumbing to biological determinism. Moreover, in his studies on sociability in 'the fabric of urban life', Park admitted it was difficult to draw a sharp distinction between the two levels. Even within the Chicago School itself, towards which ethnologists, sociologists, geographers and demographers were converging, conceptions differed as to how the two levels were related.

Diversity and uniformity

The ethnographic methodology, consisting of monographs on neighbourhoods, participatory observation and life-story analysis, that was used to investigate social interaction provided the basis for a microsociology based on the subjective experience of actors in society. It was in tune with the American philosophy of pragmatism that inspired John Dewey (1859–1952) in the field of education and George Herbert Mead in psychosociology (1863–1931).

While pragmatism left its mark on the entire Chicago School, it especially influenced Charles Horton Cooley (1864–1929). Cooley preceded Park in analysing communication phenomena and processes, first by studying the organisational impact of transport, and then, in the wake of Mead, by devoting himself to the ethnographic description of the symbolic interaction of actors. Cooley coined the term 'primary group' to label those human interactions based on 'intimate face-to-face association and cooperation'. It is at this level that the individual receives 'his earliest and most complete experience of social unity'. It is 'the nursery of human nature in the world about us' (Cooley, 1909). In the tension between society and the individual, Cooley found this level of analysis essential for evaluating the effects of the new 'moral order' ushered in by urban and industrial concentrations as well as the new means of social organisation constituted by systems of psychological and physical communication. In this manner, he criticised unilateral interpretations of the urbanisation process which suggested that primary groups had disappeared while neglecting to take into account the interaction between the standardising tendencies of the city and the life experience of its inhabitants.

Charles S. Peirce, the founder of pragmatism and semiotics

C.S. Peirce (1839–1914) was a logician and mathematician who used pragmatism as a method of conceptual clarification to lay the foundations for semiotics or the theory of signs. The pragmatic method was a radical empiricism, hostile to any form of abstraction. Suspicious of universal truths, it promoted a concrete vision of things. Paradoxically, however, Peirce's work was frightfully abstract.

'A sign, or *representamen*, is something which stands to somebody for something in some respect or capacity.' Everything is a sign. The universe is one great *representamen*. This explains why Peirce's definition of the concept of sign is rather vague, for defining a sign required making a distinction between what is a sign and what is not. Hence, the difficulty in determining the scope of semiotics as a discipline. 'All thought is in signs,' he wrote. Thinking is the manipulation of signs. Pragmatism is 'nothing more than a rule to establish the meaning of words'. Alongside pragmatism, logic is defined as semiotics.

Any semiotic process (*semiosis*) is a relation among three components: the sign itself, the object represented and the interpretant. 'The sign,' wrote Peirce, 'addresses somebody, that is, it creates in the mind of that person an equivalent sign, or perhaps a more developed sign. That sign which it creates I call the interpretant of the first sign. That sign stands for something, its object, not in all respects, but in reference to a sort of idea, which I have sometimes called the ground of the representation.' This relation is called a 'triad'. A meaning is never a relation between a sign and what the sign signifies (its object), but rather the result of the triadic relation in which the interpretant plays the mediating role of informing, interpreting or translating one sign into another.

According to Peirce, there are three types of signs: the icon, the index and the symbol. The first resembles its object like a model or a map. It would be a sign even if its object did not exist, just as a pencil line represents a geometric line. The index is a sign that would immediately lose its nature as a sign if its object were removed, but it would remain a sign even if it had no interpretant. An example might be a plate bearing the impact of a bullet as a sign of a shot having been fired. Without the shot, there would have been no impact. But there is, in fact, an impact, whether or not someone thinks of attributing it to a shot. The symbol is a sign conventionally associated with its object, such as words or traffic signals. It would lose its character as a sign if it did not have an interpretant. From this standpoint, thought or knowledge is a

network of signs capable of producing itself *ad infinitum*. (
application of Peirce's thought to the study of media, see Eco,
1976; Veron, 1988; Bougnoux, 1989.)

The ethnographic approach itself was governed by a certain
conception of the process of individualisation or self-construction.
Individuals were held to be capable of a singular, unique experience conveyed in their life stories, and at the same time subject to
the forces that levelled and standardised behaviour. The same
ambivalence of the urban personality could also be found in the
Chicago School's conception of the media, seen all at once as factors of emancipation and the deepening of individual experience
and generators of superficial social relations and social disintegra-
tion. When communication took place, it was held to be the result
of diversity among individuals. Although individuals were subject
to standardising forces, they could still escape them. The same
tension runs through the work of Dewey, who considered communication as both the cause of and the remedy for the loss of
social community and political democracy (Dewey, 1927).

2 Mass communication research

Harold Lasswell and the impact of propaganda

The first element in the conceptual system of the mass communication research movement dates from 1927 in the form of a book
by Harold D. Lasswell (1902–78), entitled *Propaganda Technique
in the World War*. The aim of this work was to draw lessons from
World War I, the first 'total' war. Methods of dissemination appeared

to be indispensable instruments for 'governmental management of opinion', on both the Allied and enemy sides. More generally, considerable strides were made in communication techniques, from the telegraph and the telephone to radio and cinema. For Lasswell, propaganda was henceforth synonymous with democracy, since it was the only way to generate the support of the masses. Moreover, it was more economical than violence, corruption or other comparable techniques of government. Since it was a mere instrument, it was neither more nor less moral than 'the crank of a water pump'. It could be used for good or for ill. This instrumental vision established the idea of the media as a set of all-powerful tools for 'circulating effective symbols'. In the post-war period, it was generally believed that the routing of the German armies owed a great deal to Allied propaganda efforts. The audience was seen as a passive target, blindly responding to stimuli. The media were thought to act like a 'hypodermic needle', a term coined by Lasswell himself to designate their direct, undifferentiated impact on atomised individuals.

This central hypothesis was in keeping with the accepted psychological theories of the time: Le Bon's psychology of crowds; behaviourism, inaugurated in 1914 by John B. Watson; the theories of Russian psychologist Ivan P. Pavlov on conditioning; and the studies of Britain's William McDougall, a pioneer of social psychology, who claimed that only certain primitive impulses or instincts could explain the acts of human beings and animals. These various approaches developed empirical methodologies inspired by the natural sciences.

As World War II drew near, many works contributed to reinforcing the notion of the omnipotence of the media and propaganda. One of the most famous was by a Russian émigré to France, Serge Chakhotin, whose title clearly illustrates the point of view of the times: *Le Viol des foules par la propagande politique* (*The*

Rape of the Masses: The Psychology of Totalitarian Political Progaganda) (1939). The work, representing a survey of current knowledge on the subject, was dedicated by the author to his 'great master', I.P. Pavlov, and his 'great friend' and 'ingenious thinker of the future', H.G. Wells. In fact, it was Wells's fantasy novel *The War of the Worlds* that Orson Welles brought to a CBS radio audience on the night of 30 October 1938, leaving thousands of credulous Americans terrorised by the science fiction tale of a 'Martian invasion'. A team of sociologists from the University of Princeton quickly set about studying this reaction of panic (Cantril et al., 1940).

Lasswell, a political scientist teaching at the University of Chicago, was deeply interested in questions of propaganda, public opinion, public affairs and elections. His second study, *Psychopathology and Politics* (1930), analysed the biographies of reformist and revolutionary leaders whose personalities he interpreted according to the degree of their rebellion against their fathers. The 1930s offered him a perfect laboratory for studying political propaganda. F.D. Roosevelt's election in 1932 ushered in the New Deal along with new techniques for shaping public opinion. The Roosevelt administration aimed to mobilise public opinion in favour of the welfare state in order to bring the country out of the Depression. Opinion polls were created as tools for day-to-day management of public affairs. Pre-election polls carried out by the firm of Gallup, Roper and Crossley successfully predicted the re-election of President Roosevelt in 1936. In 1937 came another indication of the developing discipline: the American Association for Public Opinion Research (AAPOR) founded *The Public Opinion Quarterly*, the first university journal on mass communication.

In the background of Lasswell's studies in the 1930s lay the rise of the propaganda strategies of both the Axis powers and the Soviet bloc. In his 1935 work, *World Politics and Personal Insecurity*, he undertook a systematic study of media content and developed indicators designed to reveal trends in 'world attention', that is, the elements shaping the 'world symbolic environment', and to facilitate policy-making. He was partially successful in implementing this project in 1940–1 when he was given the task of organising the Wartime Communication Study for the US Library of Congress.

Functionalist sociology and the media

Who says what in which channel to whom with what effect? With this formula, which made him famous, Lasswell provided a conceptual framework for the functionalist sociology of the media, which, until then, had provided only monographs. Translated into areas of research, Lasswell's formula gave rise to control analysis, content analysis, mass media analysis, audience analysis and impact analysis, respectively.

In practice, two points in this programme were favoured: impact analysis and, closely correlated with it, content analysis, which provided scholars with elements for orienting their approach to the public. This research technique aimed to achieve an objective, systematic and quantitative description of the manifest content of communications (Berelson, 1952). The attention paid to the effects of the media on receivers and the constant evolution of knowledge, behaviour, attitudes, emotions, opinions and actions were a response to practical objectives. All these studies were required to yield results by sponsors who were concerned about calculating the effectiveness of governmental information campaigns, corporate advertising campaigns or army propaganda efforts in wartime.

This impact-oriented research tradition had acquired the particular features of American media research even before the demand for commercial expertise in the 1930s. In fact, interest in media impact can be traced to the years preceding World War I, when research on the effects of media on children and young people was conducted in an effort to mobilise public opinion during a period of social reform. The year 1933 witnessed the beginning of a long tradition of studies on the question of the media and violence, with the publication of a twelve-volume report from the Payne Foundation, in which a group of eminent psychologists, sociologists and educators examined the impact of cinema on knowledge of foreign cultures, attitudes towards violence and delinquent behaviour. Distancing itself from Lasswell's postulates, this research represented an early questioning of the behaviourist theory of the direct effect of messages on receivers. It showed an interest in factors that generated differences in message reception, such as age, sex, social class, past experiences and parental influence (Wartella and Reeves, 1985).

According to Lasswell, the communication process fulfils three main functions in society: (a) surveillance of the environment that provides warnings about imminent threats and dangers to the system of values of a community or its parts; (b) correlation of the parts of society in responding to the environment; and (c) transmission of the social heritage from one generation to the next or cultural transmission (Lasswell, 1948).

A fourth function – entertainment – was added by two sociologists, Paul F. Lazarsfeld (1910–76) and Robert K. Merton (born in 1910). They introduced greater complexity to the theory by discerning the possibility of dysfunction and drawing a distinction between latent and manifest functions. Applying the generic codes proposed by Merton in *Social Theory and Social Structure* (1949), a defence of functionalist-inspired sociology, the two authors conceived functions as factors contributing to the adaptation or adjustment of a given system and dysfunctions as disturbing them. This is the case for the 'narcotic dysfunction' in which the media engender political apathy among the masses. Functions prevent dysfunctions from precipitating the system into a state of crisis. Manifest functions are those which are understood and desired by those taking part in the system, whereas latent functions are those which are neither understood nor desired as such. In this interplay of functions and dysfunctions, the system is viewed in terms of equilibrium and disequilibrium, stability and instability. As sociologist Norbert Elias (1897–1990) pointed out:

> The notion of function was based on a value judgment that underlay the explanations of the notion and its use. The value judgment consisted in the fact that functions were unwittingly understood to mean the activities of a part that was 'good' for the whole, because they contributed to the preservation and integrity of an existing social system. . . . Obviously, there were articles of faith of a social nature mixed up here with scientific analysis. (Elias, 1970)

This vision, expressed after the war by Merton and Lazarsfeld, was in the tradition of functionalist approaches adopted between the wars by biologists such as Ludwig von Bertalanffy, one of the precursors of systems theory (see Chapter 3), and British ethnologists such as A.R. Radcliffe-Brown and Bronislaw Malinowski, who were strongly influenced by Durkheim. From the work of these ethnologists, Merton borrowed the postulate of the functional unity of society.

A theoretical split

Merton and Lazarsfeld both taught at Columbia University. Merton was, above all, a theoretician of sociological methods and the sociology of science, and he made fewer forays into the sociology of media than his colleague, who, while also interested in other fields, devoted much effort to this sector of the social sciences. In the history of functionalism, he is ranked among the four 'fathers' of mass communication research, along with Lasswell and psychologists Kurt Lewin and Carl Hovland. It was Lazarsfeld who founded the Bureau of Applied Social Research in 1941 at Columbia University. An Austrian émigré to the United States in 1935, Lazarsfeld had been a psychologist close to the Vienna Circle and was trained in experimental research. In 1938, he was placed in charge of the Princeton Radio Project sponsored by – and carried out with – Frank Stanton, a psychologist and director of research for the CBS radio network, who later became its chairman in the television era. This administrative research project was the first in a series of quantitative studies on audiences. Collaboration between the two men led, in particular, to the designing of a 'programme analyzer' or 'profile machine' to record listener reactions in terms of interest, dislike or indifference. Listeners expressed their satisfaction by pressing a green button held in their right hand and dissatisfaction by pressing a red button in their left hand; pressing no button indicated indifference. The buttons were connected to a setting mechanism using a stylus to record the highs and lows of listener reactions on a revolving paper cylinder. Christened the 'Lazarsfeld–Stanton analyzer', the process was originally created for radio but was soon adopted by specialists to analyse the reactions of cinema audiences.

Lazarsfeld's empirical methodology, involving repeated surveys of the same sample of people (or panels) about the effects of the media, reflected his project of formulating social facts in formal, mathematical terms. These procedures contrasted with the studies he had previously carried out in Austria at a time when he identified with socialist ideals. Indeed, in the early 1930s, he had conducted a classic sociological survey on unemployment in the Austrian village of Marienthal, using life histories and participatory observation (Lazarsfeld et al., 1932).

During his exile in the United States, Lazarsfeld stood aloof from the tradition of social involvement embodied by most of the thinkers of the Chicago School in the 1930s. He questioned the very conception of the media held by thinkers such as Cooley and Park, who, under the influence of pragmatist philosophy, viewed the media as instruments for lifting society out of the crisis and leading it towards a more democratic life. Lazarsfeld had abandoned any aspirations of being a social prophet, and adopted the attitude of an 'administrator', whose main concern was to come up with useful operating tools of evaluation for media managers whom he assumed were neutral. Instead of 'critical research', he called for 'administrative research' (Lazarsfeld, 1941). The idea was beginning to emerge that the aim of a science of society could not be to build a better society, since the existing democratic system, represented by the United States, had already reached perfection. During the post-war period and McCarthyism, anyone who entertained the idea of perfecting the system or inventing another became suspect of yielding to totalitarian temptations. This led Lazarsfeld to abstract communication processes from modes of organising economic and political power.

The changes in Lazarsfeld's thinking reflected an underlying trend in the social sciences in the United States. From 1935 onwards, the challenge to the supremacy of the Chicago School gradually gave rise to the appearance of other university centres and theoretical orientations. Foremost among them were Harvard, with the symbolic figure of Talcott Parsons (1902–79), whose work *The Structure of Social Action* (1937) was the first attempt to create a unified social science based on functionalism, and Columbia, with Merton and Lazarsfeld. Together, these centres formed a pole around which a new conception of sociology as a profession developed. Although they were jointly involved in the project of building functionalism, they did not necessarily share the same assumptions about the role of empirical research. Like his colleagues from Columbia, Parsons subscribed to the idea of social science as a 'neutral' field, that is, non-partisan and not committed to working in favour of the welfare state, since science was, by definition, demo-cratic. Unlike Lazarsfeld and his colleagues, who lived on private and public commissioned studies, the Harvard sociologist deliber-ately refrained from any form of alliance with economic power and its market-oriented reasoning, and indeed from consulting in gen-eral. This difference affected the way he looked at theory. Throughout his career, Parsons founded his project of a sociology of action on a structural-functionalist social science capable, according to sociologist François Bourricaud, who introduced it in France, of 'transcending the specific limitations of particular social sciences and grasping social phenomena as a whole, with all of their reciprocal connections – a whole no longer presented as a sum of more or less miscellaneous aspects, but rather as a system of relations determining the structure of social interaction' (Bourricaud, 1955). The richness of Parsons' interdisciplinary approach contrasted with the position of researchers like Merton who was concerned with preserving the operational character of his research programme. Merton proposed to accumulate a set of 'middle-range theories' or 'theories intermediate to the minor working hypotheses evolved in abundance during the day-by-day routines of research, and the all-inclusive speculations comprising a master conceptual scheme from which it is hoped to derive a very large number of empirically observed uniformities of social behaviour' (Merton, 1949).

The 'two-step flow of communication'

During the 1940s and 1950s, an innovation occurred in the history of functionalist sociology of the media: the discovery of an inter-mediary element, midway between the beginning and the end of the communication process. This innovation was a challenge to

Lasswell's mechanistic principle of direct, undifferentiated impact and, by implication, the tautological argument concerning the 'massifying effect' of 'mass society'.

Two leading works of research marked the emergence of the new theory of intermediaries. The first study, called *The People's Choice*, was published in 1944. Lazarsfeld, together with his colleagues Bernard Berelson and Hazel Gaudet, sought to measure the influence of the media on 600 voters in Erie County, Ohio, at the time of the 1940 presidential election. The second work, *Personal Influence: The Part Played by People in the Flow of Mass Communication*, co-authored by Lazarsfeld and Elihu Katz, was published in 1955, though it drew upon surveys carried out ten years earlier. The subject was the behaviour of consumers of fashion and leisure activities, and, in particular, their choice of films. In studying the individual decision processes of a sample of 800 women in Decatur, Illinois, a city of 60,000 inhabitants, they emphasised – as in the previous study – the importance of the 'primary group'. This led them to envision the communication flow as a process unfolding in two steps, in which the role of 'opinion leaders' was found to be decisive. This was the theory of the two-step flow. The first step involves people who are relatively well informed because they are directly exposed to the media; the second step involves those who have less contact with the media and depend on others for information.

In the electoral field, Lazarsfeld used the panel technique to study the successive phases of a decision 'in the process of being made'. This method and the assumption on which it was based could be applied more generally to the process by which any innovation is disseminated and then adopted, whether it be a machine or a type of fertiliser, a type of consumer good, a health practice or a technology. This approach oriented research towards determining the successive stages involved in such processes. Models were developed to codify the steps (awareness, interest, evaluation, trial, adoption or refusal) that served as a framework for determining the mode of communication – mass or interpersonal – most apt to bring about the adoption of the innovation.

Communication and development

In 1950, Daniel Lerner, a political science professor, was placed in charge of a joint research project involving MIT, where he was teaching, and the Bureau of Applied Research at Columbia, under the direction of Lazarsfeld. Sponsored by the government radio station Voice of America, the project was aimed at evaluating, in a politically turbulent area (six Middle East countries, including Iran under Mosaddeq), the degree to which inhabitants were exposed to the media; their opinions on local, national and international affairs; and, above all, gauging their reactions to international radio broadcasts (BBC, Radio Moscow and Voice of America). The results of this first major comparative survey were published in 1958 under the title *The Passing of Traditional Society: Modernizing the Middle East*. Lerner proposed a typology of attitudes towards 'development', which, as the title suggests, was a process of transition from a 'traditional' state to a 'modernised' state. The West provided the only possible model for modernisation, thanks to the presence in Western culture of empathy, defined as the psychic mobility proper to the modern personality, which had enabled Western people to shake off the yoke of passivity and fatalism. These were hardly innocent concepts, coming five years after the coup d'état against Mosaddeq, the prime minister who was overthrown for nationalising the petroleum industry. They tended to legitimate a particular conception of development.

In the 1950s and 1960s, a host of studies produced by various authors gave rise to an operational version of the 'theory of modernisation' (Pool, 1963; Schramm, 1964). Every one of these studies presented the way out of under-development as a linear passage from 'traditional society' to 'modern society', with all the handicaps concentrated in the former, while the latter included all the advantages required to achieve the 'revolution of rising expectations'. No young nation could abandon the values of traditional society and adopt those of modernity unless it was prepared to go through all the same phases or stages already experienced by its elders in the West.

The media were seen in this perspective as perfect agents for mobilising people in favour of modernisation by disseminating modern attitudes of mobility. Being equipped with technological tools was a guarantee of progress within everyone's reach.

During the 1960s and the first half of the 1970s, a period of intensified development of US State Department programmes and agencies as well as educational foundations, operational surveys were carried out in the service of sectorial policies for 'disseminating innovations' (such as birth control methods and farming techniques), especially in Latin America and Asia. Everett Rogers became the leading figure in this process with the publication in 1962 of *The Diffusion of Innovations*. In his view, development-as-modernisation was 'a type of social change in which new ideas are introduced into a social system in order to produce higher *per-capita* incomes and levels of living through more modern production methods and improved social organisation'. This implied strategies for research and action, typologies of target populations and the stages through which they had to pass. Peasants were divided, for example, into 'innovators', 'early adopters', 'early majority', 'late majority' and 'laggards'.

Specialists in the sociology of rural communication in several third-world countries criticised diffusionist theory for failing to take into account the rigid hierarchies and power relations within deeply segregated societies, where the decision to adopt or refuse an 'innovative idea' or the identification of 'opinion leaders' may be strongly conditioned by the mechanisms of power (Beltran, 1976; Bordenave, 1976).

These concerns converged with those of market specialists and the models were interchangeable with those used in marketing, for example the so-called AIDA model (capture Attention, raise Interest, stimulate Desire, take Action). Exchange was constant between university institutions and private research groups. The Bureau of Applied Social Research performed many studies on products from cosmetics, toothpaste and soap to instant coffee and men's clothing. Students trained by Lazarsfeld became the 'gurus' of the advertising industry. One of them was Ernst Dichter, a native of Vienna, who was considered 'the father of motivational research'; another was Herta Herzog, who was hired by a large New York advertising agency and became a major figure in consumer motivation research.

Lazarsfeld did not hesitate to debate publicly with his disciples about the methods to be used in exploring consumer behaviour (Lazarsfeld and Rosenberg, 1955). Thus, Dichter criticised him for placing too much emphasis on surveys and structured question-naires composed of so-called closed items, at the expense of clinical procedures, psychoanalysis (e.g., depth interviews) and cultural anthropology, which he believed were better able to define the 'product image' and the symbolic dimensions of the purchasing act, the 'brand image'. In Dichter's view, Lazarsfeld was guilty of adhering too much to the mathematical tradition of Adolphe Quételet and not enough to that of Freud.

Lazarsfeld's influence abroad was considerable. He conceived of his ties to the international community as a 'scientific multinational' (Pollak, 1979).

Group decision-making

The notions of the 'primary group' and the 'intermediate step' introduced by Lazarsfeld and his co-workers were a novelty in functional analysis of the media, but they were already in use in other approaches to communication. First of all, the notion of a primary group was an integral part of the conceptual framework of the members of the Chicago School. Furthermore, there was the tradition of research on the 'indirect effects' of the media on children and young people, which had resulted in the Payne Foundation report in the United States and which had a German precursor in the person of Hugo Munsterberg (1863–1916), an early experimental psychologist who taught at Harvard for twenty years. There was also the early work of Elton Mayo, a pioneer of industrial psycho-sociology who rediscovered – between 1927 and 1932 – the role played by primary groups and latent functions in the effort to achieve productivity in a Western Electric workshop. His work tended to refute F.W. Taylor's theses on the scientific organisation of labour.

But the primary hypothesis that brought about the shift foreshadowed in Lazarsfeld's early work on voting sprang most directly from the work of Kurt Lewin (1890–1947). A native of Vienna like Lazarsfeld, Lewin founded a centre for research in group dynamics at the Massachusetts Institute of Technology in 1945, after teaching for more than ten years at the University of Iowa where he had headed the Child Welfare Research Station. In 1935, he published

A Dynamic Theory of Personality and, the following year, *Principles of Topological Psychology.*

Lewin studied 'group decision-making', the phenomenon of the leader and the reactions of each member to a message communicated via different channels within the group. The encounter group could be a family or families, a classroom, a young boys' club, a work group, the staff of a hospital or a factory workshop. World War II provided Lewin with an occasion to test these laws of group behaviour in mobilising people for the war effort within an economy of scarcity. He developed strategies for persuading housewives to change their attitudes towards nutrition. During these experiments, the notion of 'gatekeeper' or controller of the information flow, a role played by the informal 'opinion leaders', took shape.

Trained in psychology and mathematics, Lewin incorporated into his studies the concepts of 'topology' and 'vectors' and made prolific use of diagrams, circles, squares, arrows, and plus and minus signs to designate or represent his 'theory of fields of experience'. The 'field' is the 'vital space', the *Lebensraum* in which the relations between the organism and its environment take form. In this life-space, individual behaviour and development are determined through dynamic interaction with the psychological and social environment. By combining the mental and physical dimensions, topological analysis studies how 'forces' or 'vectors' of varying intensities and directions condition relationships between individuals and play a role in resolving the 'tension' produced by certain needs in an organism.

Carl Hovland (1912–61), a psychologist of the learning process, was the last member of the founding quartet of functional analysis. His contribution took a very different direction from the one chosen by Lewin, adopting the behaviourist assumptions of Lasswell. Hovland, a Yale University researcher, is known above all for his experimental studies conducted on persuasion during World War II. These tests, carried out on US soldiers on the Pacific and European fronts, were aimed at measuring the effectiveness of Allied propaganda films illustrating the causes and aims of the war, their effect on the morale of the troops, the extent to which they were informed and their attitude in combat. After the war, these experiments gave rise to a set of important research projects on methods for improving the effectiveness of mass persuasion. This work involved experiments based on varying 'the image of the communicator', the nature of the content of messages and the situation in which the audience was placed. The result was a veritable recipe book for all good 'persuaders' on how to get across an effective, persuasive message, that is, how to alter the psychological functioning of individuals and lead them to perform acts desired by the sender.

Although it was originally based on a belief in the omnipotence of the media, mass communication research continually relativised their effects on receivers, but without ever challenging the instrumental view underlying Lasswell's theory (Gitlin, 1979; Piemme, 1980; Beaud, 1984). The next phase in media research would bring to the fore the so-called theory of 'uses and gratifications' (see Chapter 6.2).

A dissident voice

In the 1950s, Columbia professor C. Wright Mills (1916–62) formulated a radical critique of what he called the sociology of 'bureaucrats' and 'functionaries of intelligence'. Heralding the campus rebellion of the following decade, he was a lone voice in promoting an alternative to communication that would be 'non-positivistic, in touch with the pulse, the pace and the textures of American life' (Carey, 1983). For this reason, Mills, who died prematurely, is considered to be one of the founders of American cultural studies, which emerged at roughly the same time that the foundations for British cultural studies were being laid (see Chapter 4.3).

In Mills's view, sociology had lost any impulse to bring about reform since the end of the 1930s and had strayed into social engineering by limiting itself to 'examining fragmentary problems and isolated causal links' and taking orders from the 'power triangle' (monopolies, the army and the state) that he dissected in *The Power Elite* (1956). Mills called for a return to 'sociological imagination', the title of one of his works, published in 1959. While remaining faithful to the philosophical tradition of pragmatism and its continuation in symbolic interactionism, Mills was open to the contributions of critical Marxism. His studies restored the connection between questions of culture and power, subordination and ideology, by demonstrating the link between personal experience of everyday realities and the collective stakes of society as a whole crystallised into social structures.

Mills refused to dissociate leisure from work and define leisure as a separate problem. He rejected the neutral, self-contained notion of 'entertainment' that functional analysis had deprived of any historical specificity or cultural originality. In its place, he proposed the notion of 'authentic leisure' which would allow critical distance from the various forms of commercial culture. Authentic leisure did not turn individuals into 'happy robots' who are satisfied with their situation, despite the constant constraints exercised on them by an increasingly centralised 'cultural system'. During the same period, the basic question for which Mills sought an answer was: which type of men and women does society tend to create (Mills, 1963)? The same question preoccupied French philosopher and sociologist Henri Lefebvre (1901–91), who attempted to answer it in a pioneering work, *Critique of Daily Life,* a critical analysis of hedonistic and consumerist modernity as the horizon of human happiness (the first volume was published in 1947, the second in 1962, and the third in 1981). Mills and Lefebvre concurred in denouncing the alienation in societies represented by the superpowers on both sides of the Iron Curtain.

3 *Information Theory*

The mathematical theory of communication played a crucial role in the transposition of models from the exact sciences to the communication field. The notion of 'information', based on communication devices developed during World War II, definitively took on the status of a calculable symbol. It thus became the 'strong currency' which allowed for free conceptual trade among disciplines.

1 Information and system

Shannon's formal model

In 1948, the American scholar Claude Elwood Shannon (born in 1916) published a monograph entitled *The Mathematical Theory of Communication* as part of the research produced by the laboratories of Bell Systems, a subsidiary of the telecommunications firm American Telegraph & Telephone (AT&T). The following year, this monograph was published by the University of Illinois, along with the comments of Warren Weaver, who had coordinated research on large calculators during World War II.

Shannon, a mathematician and electrical engineer, had joined Bell Laboratories in 1941 and worked on cryptography there during the war. His work on secret codes helped develop the hypotheses found in his mathematical theory of communication.

Shannon proposed a framework for a 'general system of communication'. In his view, the problem confronting communication was 'to reproduce at a given point in an exact or approximate way a message selected at another point'. In this linear schema with poles indicating the beginning and end of the process, communication is based on a chain of constituent elements: the source of information which produces a message (such as speech on the telephone); the encoder or transmitter, which transforms the message into signals allowing transmission (e.g., the transformation of the voice by the telephone into electrical oscillations); the channel, which is the means used to send the signals (e.g., the telephone cable); the decoder or receiver, which reconstructs the message from the signals; and the destination, which is the person who or thing that receives the message. Shannon's aim was to outline a mathematical framework which would make it possible to quantify the cost of transmitting a message or communication between the poles of the system in the presence of random disturbances designated as 'noise', which were undesirable because they prevented 'isomorphism' or complete correspondence between the two poles. In order to make the communication process as inexpensive as possible, the transmission was to take place using the least expensive possible conventional signals.

This theory was the outcome of research begun in the 1910s by the Russian mathematician Andrei Markov in his theoretical study of chains of symbols in literature. In 1927, Ralph V.L. Hartley further developed the theory in the United States by proposing the first accurate measurement of information about the transmission of symbols – the forerunner of the bit (binary digit) and the language of binary opposition. In 1936, the British mathematician Alan Turing designed a machine capable of processing this information. Shannon's theory was also preceded by the work of John von Neumann, who helped build the last large-scale electronic calculator prior to the computer. The computer was developed between 1944 and 1946 in response to the US Army's search for a means of measuring ballistic trajectories, and through the work of Norbert Wiener, a former teacher of Shannon and the founder of cybernetics, which he defined as the science of command and control.

Whether the communication process involves relations among machines, among biological creatures or within social organisations, it follows a linear pattern that makes it a stochastic process, that is, a process affected by random phenomena occurring between a transmitter that is free to choose the message to be sent and the destination that receives the information with its constraints. This was, in any case, the view that researchers in many disciplines quickly adopted once Shannon's book was published. They borrowed his notions of information, transmission of information, encoding, decoding, recoding, redundancy, disturbance and free choice. With this model, the social sciences adopted the assumption of the neutrality of the 'transmitting' and 'receiving' instances. The information source, the starting point of communication, forms the message, which is transformed into 'information' by the transmitter, which codifies it and sends it on to the other end of the chain. What interested Shannon was the logic of the process. His theory in no way takes into account the meaning of the signals, in other words, how they are understood by their receiver, or the intention behind their transmission.

This conception of the communication process as a straight line between a starting point and a point of arrival was to influence very different and even radically opposed schools and currents of research on the means of communication. It was the underlying assumption of all functional analysis of 'effects' and profoundly influenced structural linguistics (see Chapter 4.2). The new complexity that the sociology of the media progressively brought to this formal model by introducing other variables (see Osgood et al., 1957; Westley and McLean, 1957; Berlo, 1960; Schramm, 1970) continued to respect this beginning-to-end schema. These variables refined but did not essentially change the model, in which 'communication' was taken as self-evident or a given.

Shannon's final model generated an approach that reduced technology to the level of an instrument. This perspective made it impossible to formulate any conceptual framework in which technology was defined in terms other than calculations, planning and prediction.

The first-generation systems approach

The emergence of the notion of 'information' cannot be dissociated from biological research. When Shannon formulated his mathematical theory of communication, the field of biology had just begun incorporating the vocabulary of information and codes. In 1943, Erwin Schrödinger (1887–1961) used it to explain the models of individual development contained in chromosomes. Since then, the organising power of the information analogy has been a part of every major invention in this field: the discovery of DNA as the basis of heredity by American scientist Oswald Avery in 1944; the demonstrations of its double-helix structure by biologists Francis Crick in Great Britain and James Watson in the United States; and research on genetic codes carried out by the three 1965 French Nobel prize-winners, François Jacob, François Lwoff and Jacques

Monod. In formulating his theory, Shannon had clearly borrowed from the biology of the nervous system. In turn, the mathematical theory of communication provided specialists in molecular biology with a conceptual framework to account for the biological specificity or uniqueness of the individual (Jacob, 1970).

In 1933, in a work entitled *Modern Theories of Development*, biologist Ludwig von Bertalanffy laid the foundations for what he would later formalise 'systems theory', whose principles provided a tool for strategic action during World War II. Bertalanffy used the term 'function' to refer to 'vital or organic processes insofar as they contribute to the maintenance of the organism'. Thus, both the systems and functionalist approaches shared the same basic concept: that of function, indicating the primacy of the whole over its parts.

The aim of systems theory was to understand the totality and the interaction between elements rather than linear causal sequences, and to grasp the complexity of systems as dynamic wholes made up of many changing relationships.

Political science was one of the first disciplines in which systems theory was applied to questions of mass communication. Political life was considered a 'system of behaviour'; the system was seen as distinct from its social environment and yet open to its influences. The variations recorded in the structures and processes within the system could be interpreted as efforts made by various parts of the system to regulate and cope with tensions coming either from the environment or from within the system; the system's capacity to control those tensions depended on the presence and type of the feedback received by political actors and decision-makers. Politics was viewed as a system of input and output, shaped by interaction with the environment, which responded by adapting itself with greater or lesser success. The responses of the system depended on the speed and accuracy with which information was collected and processed. This description of the systems approach was used by US political scientist David Easton in *A Framework for Political Analysis* (1965), a work testifying to the rise of information as a research tool in the comparative study of political systems. Another US political scientist, Karl W. Deutsch, had begun the process of appropriating information theory in the early 1950s by applying it to international relations (*Nationalism and Social Communication*, 1953). Ten years later, he presented another application of systems theory in *The Nerves of Government: Models of Political Communication and Control*.

Researchers more directly known as theoreticians of mass communication and public opinion were the next to discover the advantages of the systems model, which they applied in studies on the process of political decision-making (Lasswell, 1963; Bauer et al., 1964). The practical aim of these studies was to develop an operational understanding of some of the stakes of the Cold War: the balance of power, collective security and world government. The pressure for practical expertise was so strong that Ithiel de Sola Pool, a professor at MIT, was called upon by the Pentagon to develop a model for counter-insurgency strategies in Southeast Asia and Latin America. It was known as 'Agile-Coin', 'Coin' being the contraction of 'counter-insurgency'.

Other spin-offs of the systems model were less determined by the international context. In the same period of the 1960s, for example, Melvin De Fleur used it to increase the complexity of Shannon's linear diagram by bringing to the fore the role played by feedback in the 'social system' made up of mass communication means as a whole. 'Each medium', he postulated, 'is an independent social system in itself; but taken as a whole, the media are linked to each other in a systematic way' (De Fleur, 1966). Each of these entities is represented as having two sub-systems, responsible respectively for production and distribution; each includes a constellation of actors with their various 'role systems'. Among the actors were to be found, in particular, advertising agencies, market-study and audience-rating companies, and organisations for regulation and arbitration. The maintaining of 'system balance' was seen to condition the content. In the first half of the 1970s, Ithiel de Sola Pool further developed systems theory by applying it to the analysis of new scenarios for organising political life made possible by the development of cable television technology (Pool, 1974).

In France, Abraham Moles (1920–92), an engineer and mathematician, placed his theoretical project for 'an ecology of communication' under the banner of both Shannon's mathematical theory and the analyses of Norbert Wiener. Communication was defined as 'the action of making an organism or system located at a given point R partake in the experiences (*Erfahrungen*) and stimuli of the environment of another individual or system located in another place and time, by using the items of knowledge they have in common'. The ecology of communication is the science of the interaction of different species within a given field. The 'varieties of communication, whether close or remote, fleeting or recorded, tactile or aural, personal or anonymous, are varieties that actually react towards each other within the closed space of twenty-four-hour daily life or the social space of the planet' (Moles, 1975). Such an ecology should have two different branches. The first would take as its unit the individual being and be concerned with the interaction of its modes of communication in the temporal sphere, or sphere of time assessment, and its spatial sphere, referring to movements in a given territory. The second branch would refer to the organisation of systems of transaction between beings, the formation of connections within the logosphere, the conditioning of the planet by the many channels that put messages into circulation and the sedimentation of those messages in places of recorded memory such as archives and libraries.

2 Cybernetics

Entropy

In 1948, the year in which Shannon published the first version of his theory, his former professor, Norbert Wiener, published *Cybernetics or Control and Communication in the Animal and Machine*. In this work, he offered a glimpse of the organisation of future society based on what he claimed would soon be the new raw material: 'information'. While he looked forward to the realisation of the new ideal of an 'information society', which he called a 'new utopia' (Breton and Proulx, 1989; Breton, 1992), he nevertheless warned against the danger of its being perverted. Entropy, nature's tendency to destroy what is ordered and precipitate biological deterioration and social disorder, constituted the main threat. Only information, the machines that process it and the networks they weave can fight the tendency towards entropy. 'Just as the amount of information in a system is the measure of its degree of organisation,' wrote Wiener, 'so the entropy of a system is the measure of its degree of disorganisation; one is simply the negative of the other.'

Information must be able to circulate. The information society can only exist if there are no obstacles to exchange. It is by definition incompatible with embargoes or secrets, unequal access to information or its transformation into a commodity. The advance of entropy is directly proportional to the decline of progress. Contrary to Shannon, who refrained from any commentary on the evolution of society, Wiener, still in shock from the return to barbarianism represented by World War II, denounced the dangers of entropy and irrevocably condemned 'anti-homeostatic factors' in the form of tightened control over the means of communications in society. 'That system which more than all others should contribute to social homeostasis', he wrote, 'is thrown directly into the hands of those most concerned in the game of power and money.'

The 'Invisible College'

In the 1940s, a group of American scholars from disciplines as diverse as anthropology, linguistics, mathematics, sociology and psychiatry adopted a position diametrically opposed to Shannon's mathematical theory of communication, which was coming to be accepted as the reference in the field. The story of this group, known as the 'Invisible College' or the 'Palo Alto School' (named after a small suburb of San Francisco), began in 1942 under the impetus of anthropologist Gregory Bateson, who joined forces with Birdwhistell, Hall, Goffman, Watzlawick and others. Turning away from the linear communication model, they started from the retroactive, circular model proposed by Norbert Wiener. They asserted that the mathematical theory should be left to the telecommunications engineers by whom and for whom it was designed whereas communication should be studied by the social sciences using their own model. Yves Winkin has summarised the novelty of their position quite well:

> According to [the Palo Alto School], the complexity of even the smallest situation of interaction was such that it was impossible to reduce it to two or three 'variables' operating in a linear fashion. Research in communication had to be conceived in terms of levels of complexity, multiple contexts and circular systems. (Winkin, 1984)

In this circular vision of communication, the role played by the receiver is just as important as that of the transmitter. Using concepts and models taken from the systems approach as well as from linguistics and logic, the Palo Alto team tried to account for the overall situation of interaction and not merely study a few variables taken in isolation. They developed three hypotheses. First, the essence of communication resides in relational and interactive processes (the elements themselves are less important than the relationships between the elements). Secondly, all human behaviour has communicative value (relations, which respond to each other and mutually imply each other, may be seen as a vast system of communication); by observing the succession of messages taken in their horizontal context (the sequence of successive messages) and their vertical context (the relation between the elements and the system), it is possible to arrive at a 'logic of communication' (Watzlawick et al., 1967). Finally, psychiatric disorders are a sign of disturbed communication between individuals who carry the symptoms and the people around them.

The notion of isolated communication as a deliberate, conscious, verbal act, which underlay functionalist sociology, was replaced by the idea of communication as an ongoing, social process involving a number of behavioural modes: speech, gestures, facial expressions and the physical space between individuals. The Palo Alto researchers studied gesture (kinesthetics) and interpersonal space (proxemics) and showed how mishaps in human behaviour reveal problems in the social environment. Analysis of context took the place of the analysis of content. Communication was understood as an ongoing process occurring at several levels, and in order to grasp the meaning emerging from it, researchers had to describe the way the various modes of behaviour operate in a given context.

In 1959, Edward T. Hall, a member of the group, published his first work, entitled *The Silent Language*. He based his approach to the difficulties of intercultural communication on personal observations in the field as an officer in a regiment of African-American soldiers during World War II, and, later on, as a trainer of diplomatic personnel. Laying the foundations for proxemics, Hall's book highlighted the various languages and codes, the 'silent languages' that characterise every culture: the languages of time, space, material possessions, modes of friendship and of reaching agreement. All these informal languages are the source of 'culture shock', the incomprehension and misunderstanding arising between people with different codes, who, for example, attribute different symbolic meanings to the rules of spatial or temporal organisation.

It was not until macrosociological models came under fire in the 1980s and sociologists returned to the analysis of proximity that the decisive contribution of all the members of the Palo Alto School to the theory of communication as interaction was finally recognised.

'One cannot not communicate'

In 1977, Paul Watzlawick discussed the meaning of some of his analyses in an interview with Carol Wilder, published in the *Journal of Communication* (vol. 28, no. 4, 1978).

Wilder: The first axiom in *Pragmatics* – 'One cannot not communicate' – has a fine aesthetic ring to it and brings to mind some of the tacit dimensions of communication, but some have argued that it expands the boundaries of what constitutes communication beyond any useful or meaningful grounds.

Watzlawick: Yes, this has been said. And it usually boils down to the question: 'Is intentionality an essential ingredient of communication?' If you are interested in the exchange of information on what we call the conscious or voluntary, deliberate level then, indeed, the answer is indeed 'Yes.' But, I would say, if you take our point of view and say that all behavior in the presence of another person is communication, I should think you have to extend it to the point of the axiom.

To give you an example, many years ago I was at a symposium on communication in the Rocky Mountains. It took place in a resort composed of bungalows and every bungalow had two rooms. The dividing wall was rather thin and a dear friend and colleague of mine was in the adjoining room. After lunch one day I went to take a nap, but I wasn't sleeping yet when I heard him come into his side. And then he began doing something that sounded as if he was doing a little tap dance. I realized he didn't know I was in my room, but this behavior enormously influenced mine because I realized that he must have been thinking he was alone. As a consequence, I had to lie very still until he left again, because if I had moved he would have been very embarrassed. So in that situation there was an absolute lack of intentionality, but, so far as I was concerned, an enormous impact upon and restriction of my behavior.

Wilder: Then perhaps I could ask the converse question: Is there any behavior that you would not characterize as communicative?

Watzlawick: Well, if there's nobody around, you are up against the old question: 'Does the tree that falls in the wood make a noise if there's nobody to hear it?' For communication to take place, there has to be at least one other person. Yes, I would have to agree that there is such a thing as communication with what the psychoanalysts would call 'introject'. I can have a dialogue going on in my mind with a significant person in my life. But for the purposes of our work, I would rather stay away from researching it. Not because I don't think it exists, but rather because I don't think it can, in any reasonable sense, be utilized or measured or investigated. I know it's a coward's way out, but there you are.

You see, when I talk about these things, I talk about them as somebody who wants to do therapy. I'm not primarily interested in the purely esoteric aspects of something. What interests me is its usefulness.

4 The Culture Industry, Ideology and Power

Functionalist sociology viewed the media – the new tools of modern democracy – as playing a decisive role in regulating society and hence could only advocate a theory in which they reproduced the social system's dominant values – in other words, the status quo. Schools of critical thought began in turn to question the consequences of the development of these new means of cultural production and transmission, refusing to take for granted that democracy would necessarily benefit from these technical innovations. While communication media had been described and accepted by functional analysis as mechanisms of adjustment, they came to be suspected by critical sociology of symbolic violence and seen as instruments of power and domination.

Inspired by an unorthodox variety of Marxist theory, the philosophers of the Frankfurt School, living in exile in the United States, were concerned in the 1940s about the direction that culture was taking. Twenty-odd years later, the structuralist movement that arose in France countered the empirical method with a new emphasis on ideology. In Great Britain, also during the 1960s, the Birmingham group founded cultural studies.

1 Critical theory

The question of method

Under the Weimar Republic, a few intellectuals, including philosopher Max Horkheimer and economist Friedrich Pollock, founded the 'Institute for Social Research', affiliated with the University of Frankfurt. It was the first research institution in Germany with an avowedly Marxist orientation. Its early studies dealt with the capitalist economy and the history of the labour movement. In 1930, Horkheimer (1895–1973), who had just been offered the chair of social philosophy at the university, became head of the Institute and imparted a new direction to its research programme. The Institute undertook a critique of the political practices of the two German labour parties (the Communists and the Social Democrats), paying particular attention to their 'economistic' perspective. The Marxist method of interpreting history was modified by using tools borrowed from the philosophy of culture, ethics, psycho-sociology and 'depth psychology'. The aim of the project was to establish the relation between Marx and Freud.

During the same period, the Austrian psychoanalyst Wilhelm Reich, working in isolation, developed his research on the mass psychology of fascism, which constituted the first Freudian-Marxist approach to the mechanisms of manipulation through symbols in authoritarian regimes (Reich, 1933). His theses were rejected by the international Communist movement and Reich was expelled from the German Communist Party.

When Hitler came to power, Max Horkheimer was dismissed

along with all the other Jewish founding members of the Institute. The Institute itself survived, since it had been financed from the beginning by businessmen from the Jewish community, and its collections were transferred to the Netherlands. Annexes were set up in Geneva, London and Paris, but the sole institution destined to provide a stable location for the exiled members was New York's Columbia University, which gave them a building where Max Horkheimer, Leo Löwenthal and, starting in 1938, Theodor Adorno (1903–69) were able to continue their research.

Adorno, who was as much a musicologist as a philosopher, accepted the invitation of Paul Lazarsfeld to collaborate on a research project dealing with the cultural effects of radio music programmes, under the aegis of the Princeton Office of Radio Research, one of the first institutions for ongoing analysis of communication media. This project, the Institute's first in the United States, was financed by the Rockefeller Foundation. Lazarsfeld hoped that this collaborative effort would result in 'a convergence between European theory and American empiricism'. He expected critical research to 'revitalise' administrative research. His hopes were frustrated when the joint project ended in 1939. The opposition between the two men's mentalities proved to be insurmountable. Adorno refused to limit himself to the list of questions proposed by the project sponsor because, he claimed, it confined the object of research to the commercial radio system existing at the time in the United States, thereby preventing the 'analysis of this system, its cultural and sociological consequences and social and economic presuppositions'. In short, the questions deliberately ignored the 'who', the 'how' and the 'why'. Later on, Adorno recalled: 'When I was confronted with the demand to "measure culture", I reflected that culture might be precisely that condition that excludes a mentality capable of measuring it' (Adorno, 1969).

Horkheimer shared Adorno's feeling of profound incompatibility in terms of epistemology: 'The need to limit oneself to absolutely certain data, the tendency to discredit any research on the essence of phenomena as "metaphysics", may force empirical social research to restrict itself to the non-essential in the name of that which cannot be a source of controversy. All too often the objects of research are imposed by the methods available, whereas the methods should be adapted to the object' (Horkheimer, 1972).

The culture industry

In his study on radio music programmes, Adorno criticised the position of music, reduced to the status of ornamenting everyday life, and denounced what he called the 'fraudulent happiness of affirmative art', that is, art integrated into the system. His analyses of jazz symbolised a position which some critics saw as extreme, detecting in it a blatant European ethnocentricity. Rejecting all purely aesthetic analysis in favour of psycho-sociological criticism, Adorno scornfully brushed aside any claim on the part of jazz to be an expression of liberation. In his view, the primary social function of jazz was to reduce the distance separating the alienated individual from the affirmative culture. In other words, jazz belonged to a culture that did not encourage resistance, as it should, but rather integration into the status quo.

In the 1940s, Adorno and Horkheimer created the concept of the culture industry. They analysed the industrial production of cultural goods as a global movement producing culture as a commodity. Cultural products – films, radio programmes and magazines, etc. – all manifested the same technological rationality, the same organisational schemes and managed planning as the mass production of automobiles or urban renewal projects. 'Something has been planned for everyone so that nobody can escape from it,' they wrote. All sectors of production were standardised and this was also true for each sector in relation to the others. Contemporary civilisation made everything look alike. In every instance, the culture industry supplied standardised goods to satisfy myriad demands that were identified as distinctions which production standards had to meet. From industrial production there resulted a mass culture made up of a series of objects obviously bearing the stamp of the culture industry: serialised production, standardisation and the division of labour. This situation was the result not of a law of technological evolution as such, but rather of technology's function in the modern economy. 'In our times, technical rationality is domination itself. The basis on which technology acquires power over society is the power of those whose economic hold over society is greatest . . .' (Adorno and Horkheimer, 1944). Technological rationality is the 'coercive character' of alienated society.

The culture industry inevitably brought about the bankruptcy of culture, reducing it to a mere commodity. Putting a price-tag on a cultural act abolished its critical power and dissolved any trace of authentic experience it might possess. Industrial production made unavoidable the deterioration of the philosophical and existential role of culture.

However incisive Adorno and Horkheimer may have been in analysing cultural phenomena, they seem to have perceived only one aspect – albeit a fundamental one – of the conjunction between art and technology. Their overestimation of art as the source of revolutionary ferment kept them from perceiving other, very different aspects of this conjunction. This becomes obvious in the essay by another member of the Frankfurt School, Walter Benjamin (1892–1940), entitled 'The Work of Art in the Age of Mechanical Reproduction', written in 1933, some ten years before that of Adorno and Horkheimer. In this work, Benjamin demonstrated why the cinema could only exist in an era of mechanical reproduction as opposed to simple production of unique works. In his view, the very principle of mechanical reproduction rendered the old conception of what he calls 'auratic' art obsolete. Adorno and Horkheimer may also have stigmatised mass culture because the process of manufacturing it undermined a certain notion of art as sacred. Indeed, it is difficult not to see their writing as a vigorous protest of learned men against the intrusion of technology into the world of culture. The stumbling block indeed appears to be the 'reproducibility' of cultural objects by technological means as discussed by Benjamin. The industrial mode of cultural production threatened to result in standardisation in the name of economic profitability and social control. This legitimate criticism of the cultural industry was nevertheless too closely linked to their nostalgia for cultural experience free from any relation to technology.

Despite Adorno's entreaties, Walter Benjamin could not bring himself to leave Europe. He spent most of his exile in Paris before going to Spain, where, hunted down by the French police, he finally committed suicide. He remains an original thinker within the Frankfurt School. While Adorno and Horkheimer left their mark on several generations of intellectuals through their analysis of culture and technological civilisation, by the end of the 1970s their influence had waned. Benjamin's writings, on the other hand, became the subject of renewed interest in the 1980s, particularly the huge unfinished work he was writing during his Parisian exile, *Das Passagen-Werk*, in which Paris is portrayed as 'the capital of the nineteenth century'. Benjamin was fascinated by the century as well as the city because in them there appeared – charged with meaning like the glass-roofed galleries allowing strollers to move from one street to another – the material forms of industrial culture: wrought-iron architecture, universal exhibitions and serialised novels. Like Siegfried Kracauer (1889–1966), whose intellectual itinerary coincided with or preceded his, Benjamin concentrated on observing details, fragments, the 'refuse of history', in order to reconstruct a lost whole. In this respect, both were influenced by Husserl's phenomenology and by the methodological premises of Georg Simmel, in particular their attention to surface manifestations as a means of grasping the essence of an historical period (Kracauer, 1922–25).

After the war, Adorno and Horkheimer returned to Germany and reopened the Institute in 1950. Leo Löwenthal and Herbert Marcuse, two other famous members of the Frankfurt School, remained in the United States, where they enjoyed quite different destinies. Löwenthal distinguished himself in the analysis of mass culture with a study on biographies in popular magazines (1944) that has become a classic. From 1949 to 1954, he was in charge of the 'radio program evaluation' sector of the International Broadcasting Service, under the authority of the State Department. In this position he became involved in studies on the Voice of America during the Cold War period (see Chapter 2.2).

Technological rationality

The philosopher Herbert Marcuse (1898–1979) was without doubt the most renowned figure in the Frankfurt School during the 1960s, so much so that during the Parisian student rebellion in May 1968 young people referred to the '3 Ms': Marx, Mao and Marcuse.

One-Dimensional Man, first published in 1964, had a direct influence on the ideological struggles of the time. An unyielding critic of bourgeois culture and civilisation as well as historic working-class organisations, Marcuse, a professor at Brandeis University and later at the University of California at San Diego, sought to reveal the new forms of political domination. Beneath the apparent rationality

of a world increasingly shaped by technology and science, he perceived the irrationality of a model of social organisation which,
instead of freeing individuals, actually condemned them to servitude. Technological rationality or instrumental reason had reduced
speech and thought to a single dimension, establishing a congru-
ence between the thing and its function, reality and appearance,
essence and existence. This 'one-dimensional society' had abolished the distance required for critical thought. One of the most
incisive chapters of Marcuse's book discusses 'one-dimensional
language' and frequently refers to media discourse.

Adorno and Horkheimer's book *Dialectic of Enlightenment*,
which contains a chapter on industrial production of cultural goods,
and Marcuse's *One-Dimensional Man* together demonstrate the
profound coherence of a school of thought that spoke out against
a world in which the instrumentalisation of things had turned into
that of individuals.

Jürgen Habermas (born in 1929), a German philosopher and
heir to this current of critical thought, developed his own theory of
technological rationality in answer to Marcuse in *Technik und
Wissenschaft als Ideologie* (*Technology and Science as 'Ideology'*)
(1968). Six years earlier, he had written *Strukturwandel der
Öffentlichkeit* (translated into English much later, in 1989, as
*Structural Transformation of the Public Sphere: An Inquiry into a
Category of Bourgeois Society*), which provided the necessary background for his theses on 'rationalisation'.

In *Transformation of the Public Sphere*, Habermas pursued the
work begun by the Frankfurt School in philosophy and to a lesser
extent in sociology (theory of mass culture, studies on the authoritarian personality) by describing the historical framework in
which the public sphere began its decline following the constitution of 'public opinion' in England at the end of the seventeenth
century and a hundred years later in France. This public sphere

was characterised as a mediating space between the state and society, allowing public discussion in which both sides recognised the power of reason and the richness derived from the exchange of arguments between individuals, the confrontation of ideas and enlightened opinion (*Aufklärung*). The principle of publicity was defined as placing information at the disposal of public opinion in the general interest. The development of market laws and their intrusion into the sphere of cultural production replaced reason, that is, the principle of publicity and public communication (*Publizität*), with forms of communication increasingly inspired by a commercial model of 'manufacturing of opinion'. Habermas viewed this process as a 'refeudalisation' of society. In the process, he adopted the arguments of Adorno and Horkheimer on the manipulation of opinion and standardisation, massification and atomisation of the public. In his analysis, the citizen tends to become a consumer characterised by emotional and acclamatory behaviour while public communication dissolves into 'attitudes, stereotyped as always, of isolated reception'.

Marcuse and the Frankfurt School formulated their analyses of the rise of instrumental reason in abstract philosophical terms. For Marcuse, the question of a possible alternative to the totalising of the life-world by technological rationality or a reconciliation between *Aufklärung* and science could be envisaged only if science and technology were completely revolutionised. In analysing the institutional forms taken by the rationalisation process, Habermas placed the problem of science in the same socio-political context. For Marcuse, as for Adorno and Horkheimer, the full emancipating potential of science and technology served no other purpose than to help reproduce the system of domination and servitude. Habermas, for his part, reflected on an alternative to the degeneration of politics promoted by the state-subject, which reduced problems solely to their technological aspects requiring rational management. In his view, the solution lay in restoring the plurality of forms of communication within a public sphere broadened to include the whole of society. It was from this same perspective that he took an interest, while working on *Technology and Science as 'Ideology'*, in the student movement in California and the role played by its forms of communication in reconquering individual autonomy. Moreover, in *Transformation of the Public Sphere*, he discussed, however allusively, the rapidly expanding consumer movements in the United States.

The 'Apocalyptics' and the 'Integrated'

In the 1950s and early 1960s, a few American authors left their mark on the discussion concerning the question of the culture industry, mass culture and mass society. Among them were Dwight MacDonald, Edward Shils and Daniel Bell. *Apocalliti e Integrati* (1964) is the title of a book by Umberto Eco which summarised the split between partisans and opponents of mass culture. This work was an important contribution, even if the Italian semiologist did oversimplify the issues. The 'Apocalyptics' were those who saw this new phenomenon as threatening to bring about a crisis of culture and democracy. The 'Integrated' were those who took delight in the democratised access to leisure culture for the 'millions'.

MacDonald, a former Trotskyist, inspired by the contraction 'Proletkult', coined the terms 'Masscult' and 'Midcult' to criticise mass culture and the intellectual vulgarity of its consumers, seeing no other way out than to elevate literary taste (MacDonald, 1944, 1963). At the opposite end of the spectrum, Edward Shils considered the arrival of this new culture as a guarantee of progress. Out of this controversy arose a tripartite conception of culture shared by the various authors, even though they defined the terms in different ways.

In his discussion of aesthetic, intellectual and moral criteria, Shils drew a distinction between 'superior' or 'refined' culture, 'mediocre' culture and 'coarse' or 'brutal' culture. The first level was characterised by the serious subjects and important problems with which it dealt, as well as its penetrating, coherent and subtle way of expressing the range of human emotions. The second was less original and more imitative, borrowing genres from superior culture while possessing its own, such as musical comedy. Brutal culture was the type with the least symbolic content and very little originality.

Unlike MacDonald, who thought that high culture had already been swept away in the tide of the other two, Shils noted that there was constant mixing among the three levels and that brutal culture had not undermined the foundations of the world of superior culture. On the contrary, he noted, superior culture was attracting more and more followers, and, along with it, the high intelligentsia: 'the oldest stratum of Western society, with a set of continuous traditions, [...] despite changes in society, in the modes of financial support and in the organisation of intellectual life, is consistently reproducing and increasing' (Shils, 1960).

The debate between the 'apocalyptic' MacDonald and the 'integrated' Shils in fact overshadowed a deeper one. The discussion of mass culture was intimately related to the question of mass society, which, from the point of view of 'integrated' intellectuals, was tantamount to the end of class society and class struggle. In the 1970s, Shils, a political scientist, moved away from the debate on the nature of mass society, embodied by Western industrial democracy, well-being and growth, towards a debate on the end of ideology and the twilight of committed intellectuals (Shils, 1972).

Of the three sociologists, Daniel Bell remained most consistently in line with end-of-ideology thinking. He was among the first to combat the radical critics of the time, like MacDonald, whose Trotskyist convictions he had shared in his youth, pointing out the ineluctable contradiction facing them: they were condemned to rage against the manifestations of mass culture and society while at the same time being forced, by the very structure of the system in which they were living, to work for the culture industry. In 1962, Bell published *The End of Ideology*. Before the decade was out, he had launched the concept of 'post-industrial society', signifying the advent of a new society built on intelligence technologies and the industry of information, the raw material of the future.

---

2 Structuralism

A linguistic theory

Structuralism extends the application of the theories of a school of linguistics to other disciplines in the human and social sciences (anthropology, history, literature, psychoanalysis).

The three courses on linguistics given by Ferdinand de Saussure (1857–1913) between 1906 and 1911 at the University of Geneva are recognised as having laid the foundations for the methods used by this theory. According to Saussure, language is a 'social institution', whereas speech is an individual act. As a social institution, language is an organised system of signs expressing ideas; it represents the codified aspect of language. The task of linguistics is to study the rules governing the organised system that enables it to produce meaning. Since language can be broken down into segments, it can therefore be analysed. This involves revealing the underlying oppositions and differences which allow it to operate and have meaning.

Saussure (1915) dreamed of a general science of all languages (both spoken and non-spoken) and social signs. 'A science that studies the life of signs within society is conceivable,' he wrote. 'I shall call it semiology (from the Greek *semeion*, sign). Semiology would show us what constitutes signs, what laws govern them.'

Roland Barthes (1915–80) was the one who finally took up Saussure's challenge. In an article/manifesto entitled 'Elements of Semiology' (1964) which sketched the outlines of the project, he offered this definition: 'The object of semiology is any system of signs, regardless of its substance or limits: images, gestures, melodic sounds, objects, and the compounds of these substances that can be found in rites, protocols or spectacles constitute, if not "languages", at least systems of meaning.' He organised the fundamental elements of this project, valid for both linguistics and for the sciences based on them, under four headings: (1) *langue* (system of linguistic conventions) and *parole* (actual speech); (2) signifier and signified; (3) system and syntagm; (4) denotation and connotation.

Two of these pairs proved to be particularly important for the study of media discourse: signified–signifier and denotation–connotation. Language is an organised system of signs. Each sign has two aspects: one is perceptible and audible: the signifier; the other, contained in and carried by the first, is the signified. The two elements are linked to each other by a relation of meaning. The distinction between denotation and connotation was taken up in different, 'practical-mythical' terms by the Lithuanian-born linguist Algirdas-Julien Greimas (1917–92). For Greimas, the distinction is crucial when structural analysis attempts to delimit and systematise all the facts that transcend 'primary' or basic language (Greimas, 1966). All forms of ideology rely on the 'second' language of connotation, which is 'disconnected' from the first language of denotation. The focus of semiologists on the signified and connotation as well as their interest in the system that underlies appearances shows how far removed the semiological project of describing signification was from functionalist analysis of 'manifest content'.

In 1957, in a work entitled *Mythologies*, Barthes stressed the widespread 'development of advertising, the mainstream press, radio and illustrated magazines, not to mention the vestiges of an infinite number of communication rites (rites of social appearance) [that] make the constitution of a semiotic science an even more urgent task'. In the theoretical section of this work ('Myth Today'), he outlined a semiotic theory of 'contemporary myths' found in the forms of mass communication, which he defined as connotated languages. He analysed the workings of these connotations and their ideological implications in chronicles (published separately in the press before being included in the book) entitled 'The Face of Garbo', 'The Blue Guide', 'The New Citroën' or 'The Iconography of Abbé Pierre'. This was Barthes's first attempt at a formal presentation of semiotics. It explained how myth appears to make use of everyday language in order to make secondary, parasitic values (the ones characterising the petty bourgeoisie, which he called 'a sort of monster') appear 'natural' and 'self-evident'.

A French school

In 1960, the CECMAS (Centre for the Study of Mass Communication) was set up within the École Pratique des Hautes Études in Paris. Founded on the initiative of the French sociologist Georges Friedmann (1902–78), the centre represented the first serious attempt to provide an environment and a conceptual framework for research in communication. The programme consisted in analysing the 'relationship between society at large and the mass communications functionally embedded in it'. Friedmann's goal was to bridge the gap in French research in an area largely dominated by American functional analysis and to overcome the lack of an interdisciplinary perspective.

From linguistics to structural anthropology

Claude Lévi-Strauss (born in 1908) stood out among those promoting the transposition of the linguistics model to other disciplines. He explained his model in *Anthropologie structurale* (*Structural Anthropology*) (1958 and 1973) after testing it in his thesis in 1949, *Structures élémentaires de la parenté*. His analysis concerned myths as a form of language. Although many and varied, myths can nevertheless be reduced to variations of universal structures. Particular myths, called 'mythemes' (based on the model of phonemes, the vowels and consonants making up the basic units of language), have meaning only when combined. The rules governing these combinations form a sort of grammar that makes it possible to go beyond the surface of language to the underlying system of relations or logic that constitutes the 'meaning' of the myth. The focus on relations also serves to explore totemic systems or kinship relations, which become 'communication networks' or codes enabling the transmission of messages.

Lévi-Strauss acknowledged the decisive importance of his 1942 encounter with linguist Roman Jakobson (1896–1982), whose courses he took while in exile in New York. Jakobson, born in Russia, was the first linguist, along with his countrymen Karcevsky and Troubetskoy, to use the term 'structure', at the conference of Slavic philologists held in Prague in 1920 (Saussure had been content to use the term 'system'). Language is a system which knows only its own order; by respecting this principle of immanence, crucial for structural analysis, Jakobson revealed and systematised the rules governing the workings of language. His schema for all communication contains six constitutive elements and corresponds to six functions: the speaker determines the expressive function; the destination determines the conative function (which can only be defined tautologically: the function of language as aimed at a receiver); the message determines the poetic function (which includes all the major figures of rhetoric); the context determines the referential function; the contact determines the phatic function, which tends to verify that the listening of the receiver is still established; and the code determines the metalinguistic function, which is concerned with language as an object (through it, the speaker and the receiver verify that they are using the same vocabulary and grammar) (Jakobson, 1962).

The model of communication formulated by Jakobson was an outgrowth of the mathematical theory of information (see Chapter 3.1). Generalising the heuristic value of the concepts of code, encoding, decoding, redundancy, message and information, Jakobson suggested that anthropology apply the same schema to kinship systems.

In the early 1970s, pursuing his project to give linguistics a scientific status, Jakobson drew inspiration from discoveries of molecular biologists who had recently uncovered the laws of heredity based on DNA (deoxyribonucleic acid) and mobilised information theory to explain genetic inheritance in terms of 'programmes', codes and information. The Russian linguist went so far as to establish structural similarities between these two information systems, the genetic code and the linguistic code, that is, between a chemical message contained in the architecture of the cell that transmits 'orders of life' and a linguistic message. In both cases, the message contained in the temporal coding–decoding sequence is strictly linear; it is possible to reduce the relations between elements – phonemes or chemical bases – to a system of binary opposition.

Edgar Morin and Roland Barthes came to work alongside Georges Friedmann. Each represented his own particular field and research orientation. Only Barthes claimed an affiliation to structuralism. He directed a research group on the symbolic status of cultural phenomena and continued working on his project to develop 'a genuine science of culture based on semiotics' (CECMAS, 1966). Friedmann's studies on work and technology led him to concentrate on the problems of technological civilisation and its 'mass phenomena': mass production and consumption, mass audience, the appearance of leisure time and the development of leisure activities. As for Edgar Morin (born in 1921), he was the first to present the concept of culture industry in France, through *Le Cinéma ou l'homme imaginaire* (*The Cinema or Imaginary Man*) (1956), *Les Stars* (*The Stars*) (1957) and *L'Esprit du temps* (*The Spirit of the Times*) (1962). He was among the first to reflect on the importance of the media and question the values of the new culture. He defined his research at the CECMAS as a 'sociology of the present' focusing on events as sources of sociological information. Personalities as different as Julia Kristeva, Christian Metz, Abraham Moles, Violette Morin, André Glucksmann, Pierre Fresnault-Deruelle, Jules Gritti, Eliseo Veron and A.J. Greimas gravitated around the centre, along with researchers linked to the advertising industry such as Jacques Durand and Georges Péninou, who studied ways of putting the rhetorical machine to creative use. The journal *Communications*, founded in 1961, was one of their privileged organs.

During the same period, a comparable research centre, known as the A.-Gemelli Institute, was set up in Milan and operated as a foundation independent of the university. It, too, was born in reaction to the supremacy of American sociology of the media. The Italians devoted themselves more systematically than French semiologists to research on communication phenomena and mass culture, as the work of Umberto Eco, Paolo Fabbri, Gianfranco Bettetini and, more recently, Francesco Casetti amply demonstrates.

In *Le Système de la mode* (*The Fashion System*) (1967), Barthes applied his schema of semiotic analysis to fashion magazines, though in an extremely rigid way, as he later acknowledged. His interest in the expressions of mass culture proved to be less intense than his desire to renovate the methods of literary criticism. By the time of his death in 1980, the CECMAS had changed its name twice: in 1974, it became the CETSAS (Centre for Interdisciplinary Studies in Sociology, Anthropology and Semiotics) and in 1979 it was re-christened the CETSAP (with Politics replacing Semiotics).

Since the 1970s, Edgar Morin's research has been increasingly directed towards cybernetics, systems theory and the cognitive sciences. Throughout these years, two research teams continued working along the lines of the initial project: George Friedmann's group and, in the area of film analysis and theory, the group directed by Christian Metz until his death in 1993.

State ideological apparatuses and social reproduction

One of the major tendencies in structuralism involved a re-reading of the basic texts of Marxism. The French philosopher Louis Althusser (1918–90) was the most important figure in this domain. A teacher at the École Normale Supérieure of Paris, he published *Lire le Capital* (*Reading Capital*) (1965) with a group of his students, including Pierre Macherey, Étienne Balibar, Jacques Rancière and Roger Establet. Together, they launched an attack on vulgarised Marxism and on insipid interpretations of Marxism which had fallen into the trap of 'humanism', one of whose eminent representatives at the time was Roger Garaudy. The other major target was Sartrian Marxism. Starting from a critique of the notion of alienation, Althusser tried to show that this notion belonged to a pre-Marxist conceptual framework and was linked to a humanistic conception of society that saw freedom as a problem of consciousness and not as a problem of class and social relations. Thus, the bourgeoisie and idealist philosophy found their myth in the sovereign individual, pure and untouched by any form of determinism.

Althusser emphasised what he saw as the epistemological break between the early texts of Marx and *Capital*; he and his disciples detected in the latter work the basic founding concepts for a genuine science of 'social formations' (based on the concepts of structure, superstructure, relations of production and over-determination). In the 'organic totality' of the capitalist system, the individual has no more control over history than over relations of kinship. Individuals are mere points through which history passes, offering a medium for structures; through their behaviour and attitudes, individuals take part in the process of reproducing social relations within a social formation or historically determined society.

The society of spectacle

La Société du spectacle (*The Society of the Spectacle*), written by Guy Debord (1931–94) and published in 1967, marks the most extreme criticism of the affluent society. In 1957, the author was one of the founders of the International Situationist movement, which engaged in agitation not only in France but also in Germany, Great Britain and Italy. Its theses found their way to campuses in revolt in the United States. In May 1968, a high point for active criticism of the supremacy of the media, Debord was one of the leading figures of the protest movement. The following four passages (numbers 4, 5, 57 and 59) are taken from this book, which has generated a veritable cult:

The spectacle is not a set of images, but a social relation among persons through the mediation of the spectacle.

The spectacle cannot be understood as the abuse of a world of vision, the product of techniques of mass dissemination of images. It is rather a *Weltanschauung* which has become effective, converted into material form. It is a world view that has become objectified.

The society which is carrier of the spectacle dominates underdeveloped regions not only through economic hegemony. It dominates them *as a society of spectacle*. Wherever the material base is still absent, modern society has already invaded in spectacular fashion the social surface of each continent.

The levelling tendency which, beneath the glistening diversions of the spectacle, dominates society on a worldwide scale, also dominates wherever expanded consumption of commodities has in appearance multiplied the roles and objects to be chosen. What survives of religion and the family – the latter being the principal form of the legacy of class power – and thus the moral repression it exercises, may combine as if in unity with the redundant affirmation of delight in *this* world – this world being produced as only the pseudo-delight which maintains repression within itself. To the blissful acceptance of what exists may be joined, as if in unity, a purely spectacular revolt, which expresses the simple fact that discontent itself has become a commodity, wherever

economic abundance has found itself capable of extending its
production to include the treatment of that raw material.

Althusser's article in the journal *La Pensée* entitled 'Idéologie et
appareils idéologiques d'état' ('Ideology and Ideological State
Apparatuses') (1970) had a profound impact on the critical theory
of communication, both inside and outside France. In this text, he
drew a distinction between the repressive instruments of the state,
such as the army and the police, which exercise direct coercion,
and the apparatuses that perform ideological functions, referred to
as 'ideological state apparatuses'. The role of these signifying apparatuses (school, church, the media, the family, etc.) was to ensure,
guarantee and perpetuate the monopoly on symbolic violence exercised in the field of representation while dissimulating the arbitrary
nature of that violence under the mask of allegedly natural legitimacy. It was through the mediation of these apparatuses that
ideological domination took concrete, active form, that is, the class
in power (political society) exercised its influence over the other
classes (civil society).

During the same period, Pierre Bourdieu was also reflecting
on the question of hidden violence, but without restricting himself
to structuralist principles. His analysis of cultural attitudes and
practices was based on the notion of *habitus*, a term designating the
stable system of dispositions to perceive and act that contribute to
the reproduction of an established social order and its inequalities
(Bourdieu and Passeron, 1970). Society or the 'social formation' is
defined as a system of relationships of power and meaning among
groups or classes. Analysing, for example, the social uses of pho-
tography, Bourdieu showed how a leisure activity that was
seemingly free from the codes of dominant representation and

apparently offered an opportunity for free individual expression actually reinforced social codes and conventions (Bourdieu, 1965).

The mechanisms of surveillance

Michel Foucault's book *Les Mots et les choses* (*The Order of Things*), published in 1966, marked a high point in structuralist thinking. Foucault (1926–84) proposed in this work to undertake an 'archaeology' of the human sciences – not a history of the increasing perfection of knowledge and its progress towards objectivity, but rather a history of its conditions of possibility and the configurations or mechanisms that engender it. He unveiled the successive, clear-cut *epistemes* that had defined systems of thought in the formation of Western culture from the classical age to the present.

Published in 1975, *Surveiller et punir* (*Discipline and Punish*) radically renewed the analysis of modes of exercising power. In this book, Foucault distinguished between two forms of social control: 'discipline-blockade', made up of prohibitions, bans, barriers, hierarchies and separations and breaks in communication, and 'discipline-mechanism', made up of multiple, intersecting surveillance techniques, flexible procedures of control, and systems or apparatuses that exercise discipline by causing individuals to internalise their constant exposure to a watchful eye. From the notion of power as the preserve of macro-subjects, for example the state, social classes and the dominant ideology, Foucault shifted towards a relational conception of power. Power cannot be held or transferred like a thing. 'This power is not exercised simply as an obligation or a prohibitive on those who "do not have it"; it invests them, is transmitted by and through them; it exerts pressure on them, just as they themselves, in their struggle against it, resist the grip it has on them.' The effects of power should no longer be described in negative terms (exclusion, censorship, repression, masking, hiding, etc.): 'In fact, power produces reality; it produces domains of objects and rituals of truth.'

Althusser spoke of apparatuses and an abstract state; Foucault referred to 'mechanisms' or 'arrangements' (*dispositifs*) and to 'governmentality'. The term 'arrangement' refers to the idea of organisation and network. It designates a heterogeneous whole encompassing speech, institutions, architectures, regulatory decisions, administrative laws and measures, and scientific statements, as well as philosophical, moral and philanthropic propositions.

Foucault's theses made it possible to identify power–communication configurations (*dispositifs*) in their organisational form. The 'Panopticon' model of organisation, a social utopia, is used as a way of characterising the mode of control exercised by the system of television: it is a way of organising space, controlling time, continually keeping watch over the individual and ensuring the positive production of certain types of behaviour. The 'Panopticon', which Foucault borrowed from the utilitarian philosopher Jeremy Bentham (1748–1832), can be characterised as an architectonic figure of a certain type of power. In concrete terms, it is an apparatus of surveillance, located in a central tower and offering full visibility of an entire circle of buildings divided into cells in which those under surveillance, housed in individual cells separated from each other, can be seen without seeing. When the panoptic model is applied to the characteristics of television, it reverses the direction of vision, allowing those under surveillance to see without being seen and no longer operates solely through disciplinary control but rather by fascination and attraction. To account for television as an 'organising machine', the philosopher Étienne Allemand, in *Pouvoir et télévision* (*Power and Television*) (1980), referred to it as a 'reverse Panopticon'.

As for the notion of 'governmentality', it contradicts both the idea of the state as a 'political universal' and the theory of a 'state essence', that is, a model of the state engraved in stone. Refuting this conception of a single, rigorously functioning apparatus that had long dominated critical thinking, Foucault examined the everyday functioning of the state, its means of adaptation, its offensive and defensive practices, its irregularities and improvisations – in short, the 'general tactics of governmentality' – in order to reveal other forms of coherence and regularity.

Are the media anti-mediators?

The Enzensberger–Baudrillard controversy

In the 1970s, the German writer and philosopher Hans Magnus Enzensberger published an article in the *New Left Review* entitled 'Constituents of a Theory of the Media'. He criticised the inability of the left in the West to understand the dimensions of the challenge posed to traditional forms of political action and organisation by the electronic media, and more generally by the development of what he called the 'consciousness industry'. The left, he contended, had no strategy with regard to the media, for they were nothing more than an 'empty category' in left-wing theory. The left had not moved beyond the culture of newspapers and writing. As for the New Left that arose in the 1960s, it had 'reduced the development of the media to a single concept – that of manipulation'.

Enzensberger urged the left to surmount this historic handicap 'by releasing the emancipating potential inherent in the new media, a potential that capitalism, just as surely as Soviet revisionism, has to sabotage, since it threatens the law governing both systems'. Contrasting this repressive use of the media to a use that would restore their emancipating potential, he compared the two models of communication point by point: centrally controlled programme vs decentralised programme; one transmitter with many receivers vs each receiver a potential transmitter; immobilisation of isolated individuals vs mobilisation of the masses; passive consumer behaviour vs interaction of those involved and feedback; depolitisation vs a political learning process; production by specialists vs collective production; control by private owners or the bureaucracy vs social control by self-organisation. At a time when state monopolies were coming under fire, the struggle to free the airwaves and the search for 'alternative', 'community' media found a charter for their programme in Enzensberger's appeal.

Since the article was not translated into French, Enzensberger's arguments came to be known in France through the controversy initiated by Jean Baudrillard in 'Requiem pour les média', a chapter in his book *Pour une critique de l'économie politique du signe* (1972). In reply to Enzensberger, who claimed that only revolutionary action could release the media's potential for democratic exchange, Baudrillard maintained: 'It is not as a vehicle of content that the media give rise to a social relationship, but rather in their very form and operation, and this relationship is not one of exploitation but rather of abstraction, separation and abolition of exchange. The media are not coefficients but effectors of ideology. Not only are they not revolutionary in their aim; they are not even neutral or non-ideological in other areas or virtually (the fantasy of their "technical" status or their "social use value") [. . .]. What characterises the mass media is the fact that they are anti-mediators or intransitive. They manufacture non-communication – if we accept the definition of communication as exchange, as a reciprocal space in which there is speech and response, and therefore responsibility – not a psychological and moral responsibility but rather a personal correlation of one to the other in the exchange [...]. Nowadays, the entire structure of the media is based on this last definition: they are that which for-ever prohibits a response, that which makes any process of exchange impossible (except in the form of simulated answers that are integrated into the process of transmission and in no way alter the unilateral nature of the communication). That is where their real abstraction lies, and in that abstraction is grounded the system of social control and power.'

The reification of structure

Structuralism, and in particular Althusser's theories, was promptly criticised for reducing the functioning of society to a mechanical process or a theatre without players. He was reproached for overindulging in the analysis of invariants and determinisms and for tending to obliterate the action of subjects. By remaining locked inside the text, structural linguistics had reduced the context to 'code', and in the process, to use Jakobson's classification, the 'referential function' had become blurred while the 'metalinguistic function' had won out. 'Verbal context had replaced references to action and feeling in such a way that language was no longer concerned with anything except itself through recurrence or redundancy,' as Henri Lefebvre had noted as early as 1967, in his criticism of structuralism in a book entitled *Position: Contre les technocrates* (*Position: Against Technocrats*). In his view, the structural approach had succumbed to 'taxonomy fever' and yielded to the 'supreme abstraction, the perfect mental construct, tautology mistaken for fullness', elimi-nating from its reality anything 'deviant', all 'lived experience', all 'decoding through daily life', thereby reinforcing the idea of the inevitability of constraint and control and preparing the advent of 'cyberanthropes' and technocrats.

Althusser indeed had a tendency to reduce the ideological apparatus of information to a monolithic system under the control of a state totality from which civil society was excluded. The apparatus was defined once and for all. It was of little importance, in this perspective, whether the apparatus obeyed the logic of public service or commercial interest. The terms he used to characterise communication's inherent mission suggested the thesis of vertical manipulation.

When the structural theory of social relations entered into crisis at the end of the 1970s, along with all the other great explanatory systems, criticism of it revolved around the central question of mediations and the role of the subject, the social actor and the audience.

3 Cultural Studies

The poor man's culture

Early on, British intellectuals had concerned themselves with the appearance of a hierarchy in cultural forms. A version of the threefold division of culture (refined, mediocre and rough) first appeared, in fact, under the pen of Matthew Arnold (1822–88) in his essay *Culture and Anarchy*, published in 1869; a second edition was released by Cambridge University in 1935, a significant date.

The current which arose in the 1960s and 1970s under the name of cultural studies was distantly related to the studies in literary criticism by Frank Raymond Leavis (1895–1978), published during the 1930s. *Mass Civilisation and Minority Culture* (1930) was a plea to protect schoolchildren from commercial culture. Leavis thought that the expansion of industrial capitalism and its cultural expressions (which, at the time, meant primarily the cinema) had a pernicious effect on the various forms of traditional culture, both that of the common people and that of the elite. Leavis and the group associated with the journal *Scrutiny*, founded in 1932, sought to use schools to propagate an understanding of literary values. Although he was moved by nostalgia for superior culture and the great literary tradition, which he believed to epitomise the 'superior' values of the pre-industrial age, Leavis nevertheless broke away from the conservative position taken by the literary critics of his time. He was the first theoretician of English literature of modest origins to break into the aristocratic bastions of Oxford and Cambridge. He was openly opposed to industrial capitalism as a system and to the increasingly important role the media played in its expansion in Great Britain. As literary theoretician Terry Eagleton notes: '*Scrutiny* was not just a journal, but the focus of a moral and cultural crusade: its adherents would go out to schools to do battle there, nurturing through the study of literature the kind of rich, complex, mature, discriminating, morally serious responses (all key *Scrutiny* terms) which would equip individuals to survive in a mechanized society of trashy romances, alienated labour, banal advertisements and vulgarizing mass media' (Eagleton, 1983).

Along with its educational concerns, the Leavis tradition left to posterity an approach to the various forms of literary production based on textual analysis and the search for meaning and socio-cultural values, in clear opposition to the methods of the functionalist school. The tradition was appropriated, when the school system was being expanded in the 1950s, by a pedagogical movement in which an entire generation of secondary-school teachers, also of modest social origins, attached great value to the tastes of working-class pupils, in contrast to Leavis's elitist theory.

Richard Hoggart (born in 1918), a professor of modern English literature, published *The Uses of Literacy* in 1957. In this work, he described the profound changes that had altered every aspect of working-class life (work, sexual life, family, leisure). Published in the same year that commercial television first appeared and hence before it reached working people, Hoggart's work was both a paean to the traditional forms of life in working-class communities of which he was a product, in its resistance against commercial culture, and a severe critique of the same. Only a year later, Raymond Williams (1921–88), then a teacher in a training institute for workers, published *Culture and Society: 1780–1950*, in which he criticised the all-too-frequent dissociation between culture and society.

In 1964, *The Popular Arts*, a work by Stuart Hall and Paddy Whannel, brought to a close this period in which cultural critics wrote to satisfy a demand from school teachers and educators.

The Birmingham Centre

In the same year of 1964, the Centre for Contemporary Cultural Studies (CCCS) was founded at the University of Birmingham, a centre for doctoral-level studies on 'cultural forms, practices and institutions and their relations to society and social change'. Richard Hoggart was the Centre's first director. In 1968, when he became deputy director general of Unesco, he was replaced by Stuart Hall (born in 1932 in Jamaica). The centre reached its high point of recognition during this period, which coincided with the rise of the New Left. In 1972, it began publishing a series entitled *Working Papers in Cultural Studies* (*WPCS*).

The Birmingham Centre acknowledged as the creators of its founding ideas such authors as Hoggart, Raymond Williams and historian Edward P. Thompson (1924–93).

Williams's book *The Long Revolution* (1965) marked a two-fold break from tradition. First, in contrast to a literary tradition that placed culture outside society, the author defined culture in anthropological terms, as a global process through which meanings are socially and historically constructed; literature and art are forms of social communication among many others. Secondly, it marked a break from reductionist varieties of Marxism. Williams advocated a complex Marxism that would allow for the study of culture in its relations with other social practices. He challenged historical materialism's thesis concerning the primacy of the base over the superstructure, which in his judgement resulted in a reductive view of culture, submitted to the control of social and economic determinations. In this respect his thinking reflected a movement of ideas that concerned the entire left-wing intelligentsia in Europe, of which the philosophers of the Frankfurt School were the precursors. Early in his works, Williams criticised technological determinism. In all his works in this field, he studied the concrete historical forms taken by media institutions, television, the press and advertising (Williams, 1960, 1974, 1981).

In *The Making of the English Working Class* (1968), E.P. Thompson engaged in a controversy with Williams over *The Long Revolution*. He reproached him for remaining too dependent on the evolutionist literary tradition, which always referred to culture in the singular, whereas historians had shown that cultures exist in the plural and that history is made up of struggles, tensions and conflicts between cultures and ways of living – conflicts closely linked to class cultures and processes of class formation.

The Centre's conceptual matrix was enriched by many influences. The first of these was social interactionism from the Chicago School, which responded to the desire of some researchers at the Centre to work at the ethnographic level, analysing values and lived meanings, the behaviour of diverse group cultures with respect to the dominant culture, and the ways in which social actors define their own situations and life conditions. This interactionist tradition converged with the British ethnographic tradition, which had changed the way history was written by starting from 'below', setting up oral history workshops and joining in the work of feminists on the history of women.

In search of a heterodox Marxism, they reread the literary history studies of the Hungarian thinker Georg Lukács and the philosophical work of his youth, *History and Class Consciousness* (1923), and the works of the Russian philosopher and literary theorist Mikhail Bakhtin on Marxism and the philosophy of language (1929), as well as his historical analyses of expressions used in popular culture. They translated Walter Benjamin; discovered *Le Dieu caché: étude sur la vision tragique dans les 'Pensées' de Pascal et dans le théâtre de Racine* (*The Hidden God*) (1959), by the sociologist of literature Lucien Goldmann, and 'Questions de méthode' (*The Problem of Method*) by Jean-Paul Sartre, written in 1957 and published in 1960. They shared Louis Althusser's questions about the nature of ideology, no longer conceived as the mere 'reflection' of the material base, but as playing an active role in social reproduction. With Roland Barthes, they became interested in the specific features of the cultural and adopted a methodology based on linguistic theory to deal with a problem that was crucial at the time: 'ideological readings'. The analysis of women's magazines, television fiction and news programmes and the discourses of the press made up the core of the Centre's research programme.

The work of Italian Marxist Antonio Gramsci, who died in prison under the fascist regime in 1937, had a greater influence on the Centre than on comparable groups in France. Gramsci's contribution lay above all in his conception of hegemony as the capacity of a social group to exercise intellectual and moral direction over society and to build a new system of social alliances or 'historical bloc' to support its aims. The notion of hegemony took the place of the notion of the dominant class whose power lay entirely in the ability to control the sources of economic power. In the analysis of power, the notion of hegemony introduced the necessity of considering negotiations, compromises and mediations. Gramsci's concept of hegemony manifested his early refusal to consider cultural and ideological questions mechanically in terms of class and the economic base and brought to the fore the question of civil society as distinct from the state.

The Birmingham Centre appropriated all these influences in a critical fashion. The originality of its approach consisted in setting up study groups to focus on various areas of research, for example ethnography, media studies, theories of language and subjectivity, literature and society, and in linking its work to the issues raised by social movements, particularly feminism. The Centre soon began studies on representations of women and the ideology of femininity. This research, conducted in 1968 and 1969, revealed the Centre's interest in Lévi-Strauss's studies on myth and the early work of Barthes. Despite the significant influence of French thinkers on the methodologies and conceptual framework of cultural studies, no organic link was established at the time across the two sides of the Channel.

Towards the study of reception

Stuart Hall's work on the ideological role of the media and the nature of ideology represents a significant step in forging a theory capable of refuting the postulates of North American functional analysis and laying the foundations for a new form of critical research on the media.

In his article 'Encoding/Decoding' (written circa 1973), Hall divided the television communication process into four distinct phases – production, circulation, distribution/consumption and reproduction – each having its own procedures and its own forms and conditions of existence, yet connected with the others and determined by institutional power relations. The audience is at once the receiver and the source of the message, since the schemata of production – the encoding phase – correspond to the image the television institution has of the audience, as well as to professional codes. On the audience side, Hall defined three types of decoding: dominant, oppositional and negotiated. The first corresponds to the hegemonic points of view, which appear as natural, legitimate and inevitable – the common sense of the social order and the professional world. The second interprets the message in another frame of reference, that of a contrary vision of the world (e.g., by translating 'national interest' into 'class interest'). The negotiated code is a mixture of elements of opposition and adaptation – a mixture of contradictory logics, adhering partially to dominant meanings and values but also deriving arguments from lived situations, for example the interests of specific social categories, in order to refute widely held definitions. This article set the direction for much of the research on television at the Centre.

Everyday Television: Nationwide (1978) by Charlotte Brunsdon and David Morley, the result of research financed by the British Film Institute (BFI), marked a turning point in media studies. After analysing general news programmes and current affairs programmes conceived for an elite audience, they went on to examine so-called 'political communication' programmes, intended for a wider, more heterogeneous audience in term of class and gender, such as the programme *Nationwide*. This was the starting point for the study of popular genres such as situation comedies, sports presentations, variety shows, soap operas and detective series. *Everyday Television* sought to explore the way these mass entertainment programmes handled the contradictions in the lives of men and women from a broad range of social groups and took part in building a popular common sense. At the core of this research orientation was the study of representations of masculine and feminine genders, social classes and ethnic groups.

The next stage (see Chapter 6.2) represented an even more pronounced shift from the study of texts to the study of audiences.

5 *Political Economy*

The political economy of communication began developing in the 1960s. It first took the form of a questioning about the unbalanced flows of information and cultural products between countries located on opposite sides of the line of demarcation of 'development'.

Beginning in 1975, the political economy approach started making headway by changing the focus of thought from the 'cultural industry' to 'cultural industries'. The shift from the singular to the plural reflects the abandonment of an overly generic vision of systems of communication. At a time when governmental policies of cultural democratisation and the ideas of public service and public monopolies began confronting commercial logic in an increasingly international market, this approach made it possible to delve into the complexity of these various industries in order to grasp the growing process by which cultural activities became objects of valorisation by capital.

1 Cultural dependence

Global integration and unequal exchange

Marx and his successors spoke of the 'revolutionary' nature of capitalism and saw its law of survival as lying in the continual disruption of the forces of production. Through continual expansion and progress, this system unknowingly generates the conditions of its own downfall by developing social forces and sharpening contradictions. The 'development' of each particular society depends first of all on the evolution of its internal structures. Every society necessarily goes through certain stages and the history of each one corresponds to a pattern of succession.

To replace this vision of history, economists and historians proposed a synchronic, simultaneous model, objecting that, in many countries, the history of capitalism did not fit this schema and that 'development' was not inevitable. On the contrary, in their view, many regions of the world instead experienced the 'development of under-development'. The unit of analysis of modern capitalism could no longer be national society but rather the 'world-system', of which nations were only components. This hypothesis about global integration, put forward by economist Paul Baran in 1957 in his *The Political Economy of Growth*, coincided with that of historian Immanuel Wallerstein, who was engaged in a permanent dialogue with Fernand Braudel's concept of 'world-economy'.

The concept of 'world-economy' was defined in terms of a threefold reality: a given geographical space, the existence of a pole or 'world-centre'; intermediate zones around this central point; and very wide outlying areas that, in the international division of labour, were subordinate to and dependent upon the needs of the centre. This schema of relations may be referred to as 'unequal exchange'. Capitalism is a process of creating inequality on a worldwide scale

(Wallerstein, 1983) and it cannot be conceived other than in a vast, 'universalistic' sphere. The map of commercial networks, of which communication networks are an essential part, manifests this same centripetal configuration of the world, with its hierarchies and the coexistence of different modes of production.

The political economy of communication, which resulted from a break with the theses on the history of modern capitalism drawn from classical Marxist texts, also departed from the East/West schema that characterised US sociology of the media. The polarisation engendered by the Cold War affected the divisions within the social sciences of communication. Paul Lazarsfeld recognised this fact when he introduced his colleagues in the American Association for Public Opinion Research (AAPOR) to a new field of research called 'international communication' and urged them to strengthen their ties with the 'groups and institutions that are actors on this social scene' (Lazarsfeld, 1953). The view of the international sphere as an arena for confrontation between the two blocs or ideologies, which propelled industrial and military research and the development of new information and communication technologies, from the computer to the satellite, also mobilised the greater part of functionalist research on international communication, as administrative research on government radio stations eloquently demonstrates. The diffusionist approach to communication problems associated with third-world development and modernisation strategies could not be explained without this background of Manichean division dictated by 'national security' requirements (see Chapter 2.2). This explains why functional analysis accepted the US State Department's doctrine on the 'free flow of information', modelled on the inviolable principle of the free flow of goods, thereby defining freedom of expression itself purely and simply as the free commercial expression of private market players.

Cultural imperialism

This new view of the global sphere led to renewed studies on international relations in cultural and communication matters. It gave rise to a number of studies illustrating the unequal exchange of various cultural products.

In the United States, then involved in the Southeast Asian wars and other, anti-insurrectional struggles in many third-world countries, the issue of cultural dependence provided a foundation for the thinking of the sociologist Herbert Schiller. His first work, *Mass Communications and American Empire*, published in 1969 (actually a collection of articles that began appearing in 1965), initiated a long series of studies beginning with research on the interpenetration between the military-industrial complex and the communications industry, leading to a round denunciation of the growing privatisation of the public sphere in the United States. Thomas Guback, a professor at the University of Illinois, also published a book in 1969 entitled *The International Film Industry*, which has become a classic analysis of the strategies used by American film companies since 1945 to penetrate the European market. Schiller, a University of California professor close to the tradition begun by C. Wright Mills, defined 'cultural imperialism' – a concept which prompted both research and action – as follows:

> The concept of cultural imperialism today (1976) best describes the sum of processes by which a society is brought into the modern world system and how its dominating stratum is attracted, pressured, forced, and sometimes bribed into shaping social institutions to correspond to, or even promote, the values and structures of the dominant center of the system. (Schiller, 1976)

The Journal of Communication, one of the most prestigious specialised journals in the United States, was founded in 1950. It took on a new orientation under the direction of George Gerbner, a professor at the University of Pennsylvania, who opened it up to debates on the major worldwide imbalances in communication and changes in theoretical approaches to the subject (Gerbner, 1983).

During the 1970s, the perspective of American critics was enriched by the contribution of Stuart Ewen, who published a history of the advertising system, *The Captains of Consciousness* (1976), which remains one of the few studies on the foundations of the ideology of consumption associated with a certain idea of democracy.

In Britain, Peter Golding of the University of Leicester undertook a radical critique of modernisation theories applied to communication. Jeremy Tunstall demonstrated that the organisational matrix of the media in the world was basically controlled by the United States, while J.O. Boyd-Barrett and Michael Palmer scrutinised the major international press agencies. In Finland, the issue of cultural dependence generated studies on the international flow of television programmes (Nordenstreng and Varis, 1974), while in the Netherlands, it gave rise to research on the corporate village and the socio-cultural values of the 'industrial-communication complex' (Hamelink, 1977). The question of news flows gave rise to the theoretical works of the Norwegian sociologist Johan Galtung on the forms of imperialism (1971).

In Latin America, a region that lay at the core of controversies over development strategy in the confrontation between North and South, intellectuals gave impetus to 'dependency theory'. There were a number of variations on this theory, depending on how much room for manoeuvre was believed to be available to each nation in relation to the determinations of the world-system. The break from North American functionalist sociology, already under way since the 1960s, was definitively consummated by a generation of critical sociologists (Pasquali, 1963; Schmucler, 1974;

Beltran, 1976; Capriles, 1976; Beltran and Fox, 1980). Original attempts at social change, such as that of socialist president Salvador Allende of Chile (1970–3), added to the research agenda the politics of democratising communication (A. Mattelart, 1974; M. Mattelart, 1986).

Indeed, Latin America is generally seen as the avant-garde in this type of research because the processes of change launched in that part of the world shattered the old conceptions of agitation and propaganda, and also because, at the time, media expansion was greater there than in any other region of the third world. Latin America not only became the centre of a radical critique of modernisation theories applied to such problems as family planning, distance learning and the dissemination of innovations among peasants in the framework of weak agrarian reforms; it also produced initiatives that broke with what could be called the vertical mode of transmitting development ideals. One example of this was a work by the Brazilian theorist Paulo Freire (1921–97), *Pedagogy of the Oppressed* (1970), which profoundly influenced the orientation of popular communication strategy throughout the world. This pedagogical approach began by emphasising the concrete situation of the learner, treated as a source of knowledge in the mutual exchange between the educator and the educated. From an early date, Latin American researchers have been doing distinguished work on the link between communication and popular organisation.

Unesco and the new world order of communication

With the support of the movement of non-aligned countries, the debate on the imbalance of flows and exchanges was brought to the international community in the 1970s, a decade concerned with the 'new world order of information and communication'. Unesco was its main vector. The debate on 'one-way communication', which marked North–South relations during Frenchman Jean Maheu's term as Unesco director, gave rise to the naming of an International Commission for the Study of Communication Problems in 1977, when Amadou Mahtar M'Bow of Senegal led the organisation. The Commission, presided over by Sean MacBride, an Irishman who founded Amnesty International and won the Nobel and Lenin Peace Prizes, published its report three years later. It was the first official document released under the auspices of an international representative body to recognise and clearly state the issue of an imbalance in communication flows and to evoke strategies for overcoming it. Many studies and conferences on 'cultural policies' and 'national communication policies' were carried out in this context.

A number of factors contributed to cutting this debate short and turning it into a 'dialogue of the deaf'. First, the United States under Ronald Reagan adopted an intransigent position, seeking to impose its theory of the free flow of information at any cost. Secondly, the interests of Southern countries fighting for national cultural emancipation became mingled with those of Communist-bloc states, which cleverly used such demands to oppose any opening of their own mass communication systems. Moreover, there were contradictions within the movement of non-aligned countries itself, with certain third-world governments using this international debate as an excuse for their own failings and compromises at home. In spite of these limitations, the debate and the studies it engendered set off a cry of alarm over the unequal exchange in the flows of images and information (Smythe, 1981; Preston et al., 1989; Mowlana and Wilson, 1990; Nordenstreng and Schiller, 1993; Wasko et al., 1993; Tehranian, 1994; Schmucler, 1997). It offered an opportunity to hear the voices of people who make up a majority of the world's population and whose reality is all too often presented through the filter of studies carried out by experts from the major industrialised countries. References to the American-inspired sociology of modernisation, which predominated in international organisations, were replaced during the 1970s by representations of development formulated by those who were its subjects. Naturally, the split between the two perspectives frequently gave rise to a bi-polar vision of the world, with a dominant and domineering North and a subjugated South. Mediators and mediation processes were ignored, along with the very source of the complexity of the encounter between North and South – an encounter that Edward T. Hall referred to as 'culture shock' between individual cultures and the world sphere. In 1985, the United States pulled out of Unesco, citing a drift towards the 'politicisation' of communication problems, and was soon followed by Great Britain. In the 1980s, the issue of the regulation of networks and exchanges was taken over by more technically oriented bodies such as the GATT (General Agreement on Tariffs and Trade) (see Chapter 7.2).

2 Cultural industries

The diversity of commodities

During the second half of the 1970s, a second centre of political economy of communication appeared in Europe. The core issue was cultural industries and French sociologists played a leading role in it. In general, they adopted a resolutely critical stance.

In 1978, the research team headed by Bernard Miège published a work entitled *Capitalisme et industries culturelles* (*Capitalism and Cultural Industries*). The authors examined the nature of cultural goods and tried to answer the question: 'What specific problems does capital confront in producing value out of art and culture?' They refuted the cherished idea of the Frankfurt School according to which the production of cultural goods (books, records, cinema, television, the press, etc.) obeys a single logic. In their view, the cultural industry does not exist in itself: it is a composite entity, made up of highly differentiated elements and sectors that have their own laws of standardisation. This segmentation of the various ways of making cultural production profitable could be seen in their modes of organising labour, in their definition of the products themselves and their content, in the modes of institutionalisation of the various cultural industries (public service, private enterprise, etc.), in the degree of horizontal and vertical concentration of firms involved in production and distribution, and finally in the way customers or users appropriated the products and services.

Les Industries de l'imaginaire (*The Industries of the Imaginary*) (1980) by Patrice Flichy focused on the 'flow culture', that is, the continuum of broadcasts, typical of the audiovisual economy, in which each element is of less importance in itself than as part of the entire programme offered. Flichy was interested in both the industries of hardware (the container) and software (the content). He discussed the formation of the social uses of communication machines and the transformation of technological innovations into goods, thereby renewing the basis for a history of technologies. Previous research had analysed the intersection between the technical-economic and the political-social levels, in order to reveal the political stakes of the industry and the industrial foundations of a new system of social control. Furthermore, by insisting on the articulation between the national and multinational levels, these studies made clear the limits of the then fashionable concept of 'cultural imperialism' (A. Mattelart, 1976; A. and M. Mattelart, 1979; A. Mattelart and Piemme, 1980; A. and M. Mattelart and Delcourt, 1983).

A change occurred in European governmental circles in 1978. The notion of 'cultural industries', adopted by the European ministers in charge of cultural affairs at their meeting in Athens, was thus accepted into the administrative discourse of an important European body, the Council of Europe.

During the 1980s, the issue of cultural industries was taken up in various academic circles, in particular in Quebec (Lacroix and Lévesque, 1986; Tremblay, 1990) and Spain (Bustamante and Zallo, 1988), where a few sociologists had already laid the groundwork for critical research during the years of Franco's dictatorship (Gubern, 1972; Moragas, 1976; Serrano, 1977).

Political economy made it its task to make up for the weaknesses of first-generation semiotics, which had been attentive above all to discourse as a set of self-contained units, each with its own principles of construction. This aim of political economy, which had remained only implicit in France, became quite explicit in Great Britain, the other centre of this current. There, political economy gave rise to an open polemic with the cultural studies current, which it reproached for treating the ideological level as an autonomous sphere (Garnham, 1983). The journal *Media, Culture and Society*, created in 1979, published several contributions to this discussion.

In a provocative article published in 1977, Canadian author Dallas Smythe pointed out what he saw as a blind spot in European critical research concerning the economic logic of television. He sharply attacked theories that viewed television only as a sphere of production of discursive strategies and ideology, arguing, on the contrary, that, whatever the context, television is above all a 'producer of audiences to be marketed to advertisers', and that in contemporary capitalism, the audience constitutes the commodity form of communication products. British researcher Nicholas Garnham replied that this position was tantamount to denying the political and cultural dimension of television, which was just as essential as its economic logic (Garnham, 1979). The debate was all the more important in that it pitted against each other two different experiences and two modes of institutionalising the electronic media – the commercial regime and public service – just at the time of the first measures of deregulation and privatisation of the audiovisual media in Europe. This discussion was already under way in Italy, where early deregulation of public service had stimulated the reflection of sociologists grouped around the journal *Ikon* (Cesareo, 1974; Grandi and Richeri, 1976; Wolf, 1977).

From industrial sector to 'global society'

For a long time, the concept of 'mass society', associated with that of mass culture, was the key notion in controversies on the nature of media modernity. However, it lost its exclusive character at the end of the 1960s and was succeeded by new terms describing the way society was conditioned by technologies of information and communication. These neologisms corresponded to definite arguments, doctrines and theories concerning the future direction of society.

It was through electronic communications that the notion of the 'global' became a component of the representation of the world. In 1969, two works were published that elevated this notion to importance: *War and Peace in the Global Village* by Marshall McLuhan (in collaboration with Quentin Fiore) and *Between Two Ages: America's Role in the Technetronic Era* by Zbigniew Brzezinski. The first discussed the importance of television images in the Vietnam War, the 'first televisual war'. The authors argued that with the advent of this conflict, which every American family followed live in their homes, audiences ceased to be passive spectators and instead became 'participants', with the dichotomy between civilians and military fading away. In peacetime, the electronic media pull all the non-industrialised territories towards progress. The technical imperative determines social change. The notion of 'communications revolution' – a slogan from the United States – undermined the last utopias of political revolution. The idea of the 'end of ideology', dear to Daniel Bell, was thus relayed in collective representations. The term 'global village' began its career in the 'planetary' imaginary. The notion would be called upon at every major world apocalypse and every 'planet-wide broadcast'. The Gulf War confirmed this, even though, in fact, information about this conflict was jealously guarded by military experts.

Zbigniew Brzezinski, a political scientist and director of the Institute of Research on Communism at Columbia University, preferred the expression 'global city'. In his view, the notion of 'village' bore the connotation of a return to community and privacy and thus seemed poorly adapted to the new international environment, since the multi-level networking of 'technetronic' society through a combination of computers, televisions and telecommunications was in the process of transforming the world into 'a nervous, agitated, tense and fragmented web of interdependent relations', thus increasing the risk of isolation and solitude for the individual. In his view, the first 'global society' in history was already in place: the United States. As the main propagator of this 'technetronic revolution', US society 'communicates' more than any other since, as he noted, 65 per cent of worldwide communications were initiated there. The United States was the only society to propose a 'global model of modernity', that is, universal forms of behaviour and values, not only through the products of its cultural industries, but also through its 'new technologies, methods and organizational skills'. At the time Brzezinski was writing, in the bloc dominated by the other superpower, there were only societies of scarcity which, in his words, 'secrete boredom'. Moreover, in his view, the notion of the global city and society rendered the old notion of 'imperialism' obsolete as a way of designating the relations of the United States with the rest of the world. 'Gun-boat diplomacy' was a thing of the past; the future lay in 'network diplomacy'.

In 1977, Marc Uri Porat, an American economist of French origin, published a report, commissioned by the US government, which was the first official study to measure the weight of the information economy in US society. In 1966, information-related activities represented 47 per cent of the workforce and about the same percentage of the gross national product. These figures can only have increased since then. Porat divided 'information' into three fundamental categories: (1) financial, insurance and accounting information, stored in data bases and banks; (2) cultural information, fuelled by the products of the cultural industries; and (3) 'knowledge information', or all types of know-how (patents, management, consulting, etc.). As early as 1962, the American economist Fritz Machlup, a specialist in balance of payments studies, had undertaken an evaluation of the importance for the US economy of information activities, grouped together in what he called the 'knowledge industry'.

The 1970s witnessed an accumulation of official reports on the future of the 'information society' in the main industrial countries. In 1979, Simon Nora and Alain Minc published *L'Informatisation de la société* (*The Computerisation of Society*). This report launched the term 'telematics', which conveyed the growing interpenetration of computers and telecommunications, and suggested that the new information and communication technologies were the solution to the economic and political crisis, referred to as a 'crisis of civilisation'. Thanks to a 'new global mode of social regulation', the 'nervous system of organisations and of society as a whole' was expected to 'recreate an information agora broadened to the dimensions of the modern nation' and favour a blossoming of civil society. However, they warned against danger from foreign sources. It was an 'imperative of sovereignty' not to leave the organisation of data banks, a veritable 'collective memory', to US companies.

Gradual shifts in meaning began to take place; the notion of communication ceased to be centred on the media and took on a totalising definition, combining multiple technologies intended to organise a 'new society'. In France, the incorporation of problems raised by telecommunications into sociological studies was acknowledged in a conference on 'The Human Sciences and Telecommunications'. Organised in Paris in April 1977 through a joint initiative of the CNET (National Centre for the Study of Telecommunications) and the CNRS (National Centre for Scientific Research), it brought together researchers and telecommunications engineers along with US experts such as Marc Uri Porat and Ithiel de Sola Pool. In the proceedings, published under the title *Les Réseaux pensants* (*The Thinking Networks*) (Giraud et al., 1978), one contribution stands out – that of a young researcher named Yves Stourdzé, who died prematurely a few years later, on the 'Genealogy of French Telecommunications'. Breaking with a strictly economic orientation, Stourdzé incorporated reflections on the philosophical, cultural and institutional climate in France, which in his view accounted for the form historically taken by the government monopoly in the country. He showed how technological innovation in communications was in large part conditioned by the historical context, embodied in systems of representation of power, mental attitudes and administrative practices. The majority of talks in this conference confirmed the idea of a society that had become transparent by virtue of the 'information economy'. This was a variation on the 'technical myth' exposed in the 1950s by Jacques Ellul (1912–94), an isolated and unclassifiable French philosopher, in his work *La Technique ou l'enjeu du siècle* (translated as *The Technological Society*) (1954). Ellul returned to the same topic in 1977 in *Le Système technicien*, in which he insisted on the fact that technology, once it went beyond the status of instrument and in fact created an artificial environment, thereby became a 'system', thanks to the connections among technologies made possible by computers. In Ellul's opinion, there was an urgent need to reflect on the role of social regulation technology had begun to play.

6 *The Return of Everyday Life*

In reaction to the structural-functionalist theories which had long dominated the sociological scene, various new approaches gained ascendancy. They gave importance to new units of analysis, in particular the person, the group and intersubjective relations in the experience of daily life. These approaches caused debates to resurface which had been present in the social sciences since their inception. These included the debates on the reification of social relations, the role of the actor with respect to the system and the degree of autonomy of audiences with respect to communication systems.

1 The intersubjective movement

Ethnomethodologies

The currents grouped together around the label of interpretive sociology (symbolic interactionism, social phenomenology and ethnomethodology), which developed in the United States and Great

Britain starting in the 1960s, widened the gap between the sociologies concerned with micro-procedures and the so-called structural sociologies, which examined social constraints exterior to the individual, and established the primacy of 'society' over the subject and structure over practices.

Although the foundations of interactionism and ethnomethodology came from the work of Georg Simmel and George Herbert Mead, these approaches were built above all on the effort to supersede Talcott Parsons's sociology of action. For Parsonian functionalism, as for all so-called objectivist sociology, the action of the individual was the result of norms imposed by society and the tendency towards action generated thereby. Since the actors are assumed to have internalised society's fundamental value system, social cohesion results from shared aims and expectations. In this perspective, the 'social' is a given object. The actor's knowledge is of little importance in Parsons's work. Yet, as his study of rationality indicates, it did play an implicit role in his analyses, which assumed that actors acquire a valid knowledge of the outside world by applying logical-empirical criteria like those used in science, in a process of successive approximations. For a sociologist like Harold Garfinkel (1917–87), on the other hand, the nature and characteristics of the knowledge applied by social actors to the circumstances of their lives and the need to conceptualise that knowledge were the keys to all genuine analysis of social action. Garfinkel, a student of Parsons at Harvard who went on to teach at UCLA, laid the foundations for ethnomethodology in *Studies in Ethnomethodology*, published in 1967.

The aim of ethnomethodology was to study practical, commonsense reasoning in ordinary situations of action. In Garfinkel's view, considering the events of the social world from a scientific standpoint, external to the object, was far from the ideal strategy for treating the flow of ordinary events; it would be both useless and paralysing in the analysis of the characteristics of practical action.

> Ethnomethodological studies analyze everyday activities as members' methods for making those same activities visibly-rational-and-reportable-for-all-practical-purposes, i.e. 'accountable', as organizations of commonplace everyday activities. The reflexivity of that phenomenon is a singular feature of practical actions, of practical circumstances, of common sense knowledge of social structures and practical sociological reasoning. By permitting us to locate and examine their occurrence, the reflexivity of that phenomenon establishes their study. (Garfinkel, 1967)

He insisted on the methodical nature of practical action; the ethnomethodologist's job was to identify the operations by which people realise and account for what they are and what they do in ordinary action and in varied contexts of interaction. Ethnomethodology gave a strong new impetus to theorisations of the relationship between an action and its context (Heritage, 1987). Not only did the context influence the presumed content of the action, but actions also contributed to the gradually developing meaning of the context or the situation itself.

The social fact was no longer a given; it was the result of the activity undertaken by actors to give meaning to their everyday practices. The schema of communication replaced that of action.

Conversation analysis (Sacks, 1963) was an important component of ethnomethodology. As a privileged moment of symbolic exchange, conversation was treated as an action, no longer with a view to studying language itself, but as a language practice, in order to understand how speakers construct operations in the predominant form of social interaction, and to unveil the procedures and expectations through which this interaction is produced and understood.

Aaron V. Cicourel, a professor at the University of California at

San Diego, is undoubtedly the ethnomethodologist who has taken the most interest in the critique of the mass communication research school. Starting in 1964, in his book *Method and Measurement in Sociology*, he radically refuted the physical-mathematical-logical schema of this approach. The analysis of manifest content and the method of quantitative survey techniques were dismissed as being unable to account for the subjective dimension of the communication process. The receiver was restored to favour in his or her capacity to produce meaning and develop procedures of interpretation.

Actor and system: the end of a duality

Ethnomethodology was largely inspired by the work of the Austrian philosopher and sociologist Alfred Schütz (1899–1959). Living in exile in New York in the 1940s, he devoted his energies to studying the foundations of knowledge in everyday life. In designating everyday life as a privileged field of study for sociologists, Schütz invited sociology to investigate the 'life-world' (*Lebenswelt*), a concrete, historical, social and cultural world in which the representations of common-sense thinking prevailed. Ethnomethodology borrowed Schütz's concept of 'stocks of knowledge'; the social world was interpreted according to common-sense categories and constructs that serve as resources in helping actors to reach intersubjective understanding and orient themselves in relation to each other. These stocks of knowledge available in everyday life and in the 'life-world' are distributed differentially, creating a diversity of forms of knowledge in action and interaction, depending on the individual, the group, generation and gender. Each person experiences different 'temporalities' or 'social times', reflecting different relationships to knowledge and different positions in the networks of intersubjective relations.

In seeking to put an end to the separation between subject and object, the individual and the 'other', this approach raised disturbing questions for sociological theory. While it did not deny the need to take a distance from everyday knowledge – this was recognised as necessary for any kind of theorisation – it was essentially a practical sociology that implied a reflexive return to theory itself since it was involved in these concrete networks of interaction. The sociology of social interaction thus introduced a methodological challenge by attributing great importance to the point of view of the actors themselves in interpreting the world around them. 'Putting oneself in someone else's place' was what G.H. Mead saw as necessary to make the method of participant observation a means of generating knowledge.

Assuming Mead's legacy, Herbert Blumer founded the school of 'symbolic interactionism'. The term itself dates from 1937. Symbolic interactionism emphasises the symbolic nature of social life. In 1969, Blumer summarised the three basic premises of this approach, whose aim was to study the way actors interpret the symbols arising from their 'interacting activities':

> The first premise is that human beings act toward things on the basis of the meanings that the things have for them. The second premise is that the meaning of such things is derived from, or arises out of, the social interaction one has with one's fellows. The third premise is that these meanings are handled in, and modified through, an interpretive process used by the person in dealing with the things he encounters. (Blumer, 1969)

For the researchers of the interactionist school, deviant behaviours and extreme cases of a threatened 'self' offered a privileged terrain of investigation, since accidents in human behaviour were seen to reveal the web of the social environment and the rules constituting 'ritual of interaction'. The Canadian sociologist Erving Goffmann (1922–83) made this the constant line of his research.

His work reveals both a classical orientation and a highly original side. Taking part in the Chicago School's theoretical and methodological tradition while moving in the sphere of the Palo Alto School, he has continually combined symbolic interactionism with other approaches such as analysing the theatrical aspect of behaviour in order to demonstrate the rhetoric of everyday life: our gestures have to be true to life as in the theatre. In the course of his research, he has ventured into many fields: conversation analysis, speech ethnography and non-verbal communication (Goffmann, 1967, 1971).

Today, interpretive sociology has established its legitimacy in the United States and overcome the resistance of functionalism, which fell into crisis at the end of the 1960s. In 1972, P.F. Lazarsfeld openly expressed his fears concerning 'that strange coalition of macro-sociological Marxists and ethnomethodologists who want to explore the "real" existential meaning underlying measurement techniques' (quoted in Marsal, 1977). These currents of thought developed primarily in English- and German-speaking countries, and did not find a genuine audience in France until the end of the 1970s, when structuralism was in decline. Their arrival in France, in the field of communication sciences, coincided with the rise of studies focusing on the uses of communication devices. Among the subjects treated by the first studies of this type were interaction in telephone conversations, work meetings using videoconferencing, and videophone interaction (Fornel, 1988).

These research trends were greeted in France with a perplexity that was clearly expressed by the anthropologist Gerard Althabe:

> These sorts of projects are somewhat lacking in critical distance
> with regard to the research orientations to which they belong;
> first of all, they should emphasise their sources of inspiration (G.
> Simmel, G.H. Mead) and the meaning of their emergence and
> current development (in the past fifteen years) in the field of social

sciences and in American society [. . .]. At the same time, it is necessary to ask what meaning such orientations can have in the field
of French social sciences (in some respects, they represent a break
from the Durkheimian sociological tradition); the authors of these
studies should make clear the process that has led them to adopt
their viewpoint. The lack of critical distance often gives the impression that these studies are nothing more than imitative practices.
(Althabe, 1984)

British sociologist Anthony Giddens (born in 1938) entered this
theoretical debate by pointing out another of its components. This
Marxist-trained thinker was one of the few sociologists who early
and consistently supported Garfinkel's work, sensing that the eth-
nomethodological approach might offer a way to overcome the
split between individual and society, structure and practice. He
saw it as a way out of the schism between interpretive and structural sociology because it apprehended structure in a new way,
breaking with metaphors such as the anatomy of an organism or
the frame of a building. He proposed to replace such notions of
structure by a 'theory of structuration' that made use of eth-
nomethodological ideas on 'practical consciousness' and the
procedures of action, and thus to theorise the interweaving of practices and structure, action and institution, as well as the concrete
relationships between practices and external constraints, individual
and totality, micro and macro.

Instead of the dualism of structure and practice, Giddens preferred to speak of the two-fold dimension of the 'structural'. In *The
Constitution of Society: Outline of the Theory of Structuration* (1984),
he wrote:

According to the notion of the duality of structure, the structural
properties of social systems are both medium and outcome of the
practices they recursively organize. Structure is not 'external' to
individuals: as memory traces and as instantiated in social practices,

it is in a certain sense more 'internal' than exterior to their activities in a Durkheimian sense. Structure is not to be equated with constraint but is always both constraining and enabling. This, of course, does not prevent the structural properties of social systems from stretching away, in time and space, beyond the control of any individual actors.

The linguistic turn

Structural linguistics had neglected the speaker and the receiver. Communicative or pragmatic linguistics studied the relationship between the two and in so doing took advantage of developments in the philosophy of ordinary language (the Oxford School), the Anglo-Saxon theory of speech acts, the new Belgian science of rhetoric and German pragmatics.

Ethnomethodology was influenced by the theory of speech acts, which restored the subject, formerly excluded from structural theories of signs, as the agent of speech. The English philosopher John L. Austin (1912–60) and his book *How to Do Things with Words* (1962) were particularly influential. Austin showed that language is not merely descriptive but also 'performative', in other words, oriented to the realisation of certain results. It could even be asserted that language's true function is performative, since through the act of speaking, one can act upon others, cause them to act, or act oneself.

Ethnomethodology was also influenced by the notion of 'language games' introduced by Ludwig Wittgenstein (1889–1951) in his *Philosophical Investigations* (completed in 1945 though not published until 1953). In this work, he broke away from intellectualist rationalism and the 'representationalist' assumption of a correspondence between language and the world. Language was no longer described in its formal structures but rather in its practical uses in everyday life. The user-subject is a key determinant of language. A language game is the language-in-use of social interaction that takes part in an 'activity or a form of life'. Wittgenstein tried to understand the rules of general knowledge – a kind of knowledge that 'knows the rule', that knows 'how to go on', in other words, the practical knowledge that the user must have to carry out the routines of social life.

Aaron Cicourel proposed in 1980 to create a wide-reaching alliance of sociology, anthropology, linguistics and philosophy in the form of an 'anthropo-sociology'. Acknowledging the contribution of the new philosophies of language, his project also pointed out the obstacles that would have to be overcome for such an inter-disciplinary encounter to take place: first, the methodological problem of shifting from the analysis of very concrete speech acts such as promising, congratulating or giving orders to the analysis of complex situations of interaction; the difficulty of going from analysis centred on the speaker to analysis that takes into account receivers as interlocutors; the need to consider other 'speech acts' and other forms of communication than those allowed by natural languages (including the languages of gesture, iconic languages, etc.). A further challenge lay in how sociology could adopt and develop the notion of 'communicative competence', central to the theory of speech acts, which enabled varied 'performative statements' to be accomplished in determined communication situations. The main obstacle, however, was the lack of interest shown by linguists and by the theory of speech acts in complex forms of social organisation.

Peter Berger and Thomas Luckmann noted a similar obstacle in *The Social Construction of Reality* (1966), an important work profoundly inspired by Alfred Schütz. In this book, the authors laid the foundations for a 'new sociology of knowledge'. They observed:

The failure to make the connection between Meadian social psychology and the sociology of knowledge, on the part of the symbolic-interactionists, is of course related to the limited 'diffusion' of the sociology of knowledge in America, but its more important theoretical foundation is to be sought in the fact that both Mead himself and his later followers did not develop an adequate concept of social structure. Precisely for this reason, we think, is the interplay of the Meadian and Durkheimian approaches so very important. It may be observed here that, just as the indifference to the sociology of knowledge on the part of American social psychologists has prevented the latter from relating their perspectives to a macro-sociological theory, so is the total ignorance of Mead a severe theoretical defect of neo-Marxist social thought in Europe today. (Berger and Luckmann, 1966)

Habermas and 'communicative action'

Not only did the linguistic turn of the 1960s have an impact on interpretive sociology; it also affected the theoreticians of the sociology of action. Indeed, the new philosophies of language inspired Parsons during the last period of his scientific output, and their influence can also be felt in the work of Jürgen Habermas, who reworked Parsonian theory to develop his own sociology of 'communicative action' (1981). Action and interaction were no longer analysed merely as the production of effects, but in their association with systems of symbolic exchange and speech contexts. The attitudes and opinions accompanying an action cannot, by themselves, account for reality. Habermas refused the pessimistic view of Adorno, who saw the transformation of reason into instrumental reason as a radical perversion.

According to Habermas, critical sociology must study the networks of interaction in a society, composed of communicative relations, 'the union in communication of opposed subjects'. In place of 'strategic action', that is, reason and action narrowly restricted to utilitarian, instrumental aims (of which mass communication means constitute the privileged system), Habermas proposed other modes of action or forms of relationship to the world with their own criteria of validity: objective, cognitive action that imposes on itself the obligation to tell the truth; intersubjective action aimed at the moral rightness of action; and expressive action, which takes for granted the sincerity of the actors. He defined the crisis of democracy as stemming from the fact that the social configurations that should normally facilitate discussion and the deployment of communicative rationality have become autonomous and are administered as 'real abstractions', which do indeed circulate information but hinder communicative relations, that is, the interpretive activities of individuals and social groups. In his view, rationality is not related to 'the possession of knowledge, but to the way subjects who are capable of speech and action acquire and use knowledge'. One may ask whether the communicative relations which Habermas defines as the foundation of social relations have not been modelled too exclusively on a conception of dialogue between philosophers.

A celebrated controversy pitted Habermas against fellow German Niklas Luhmann in 1971. Luhmann responded to Habermas's theory by proposing to define a system of communication as an 'autopoietic system'. A system is a living and autopoietic one when it is operationally closed and structurally paired with the environment (see Chapter 7.1). Such systems regulate social relations as variations or circulation of meaning. Naturally, there are disturbances in communication, but these are due to the rigid workings of the means of communication or to resistance to change, and not, as Habermas thought, to any opposition between the system and the social life-world. In Habermas's view, communication is aimed at mutual comprehension and consensus, whereas for Luhmann it has no aim. It implies no discussion or debate about values. The main question concerns the control of the complexity of the system's relations with its environment as well as its own complexity. The more freely meaning is able to circulate, the more fully the system can achieve this two-fold control.

One may observe, along with Jean-Marie Vincent, that Habermas's notion of communicative rationality is 'strongly imbued with normative elements, and thus represents a meta-social principle of explanation'. On the other hand, regarding Luhmann's thought, one could object that 'interaction and intersubjectivity appear to be singularly poor, since they are reduced to relationships between undifferentiated bearers of variations of meaning, or relationships between subjects without subjectivity' (Vincent, 1990).

2 The ethnography of the audience

The question of the reader

Reacting against Saussure's linguistics and his abstract, monolithic definition of a system of language, Mikhail Bakhtin (1895–1975), published *Marxism and the Philosophy of Language* (1929), in which he presented a 'dialogical' conception of language that took into account the concrete expressions of individuals in particular social contexts. Language, in his view, can only be grasped in terms of its orientation towards the other. For Bakhtin, 'Words were "multiaccentual" rather than frozen in meaning: they were always the words of one particular human subject for another, and this practical context would shape and shift their meaning' (Eagleton, 1983). Bakhtin admitted that language cannot be reduced to a mere reflection of social interests, and hence it had a certain degree of autonomy, but he emphasised the fact that it is caught up in networks of social relations inscribed within political, economic and ideological systems. Language is a field of tensions and conflicting interests. People's evaluations of discourse and individual responses to a given statement are anything but uniform, but rather in constant transformation, according to the history and evolution of subjectivity. At the heart of the dialogical conception of language lies a radical critique of the dogmatic definition of ideology as a petrified set of general statements cut off from what Bakhtin called the 'ideology of life'.

In the 1960s, literary studies introduced the question of the reader and reception. German-speaking countries, and the Constance School in particular, played an active role. The movement was launched in 1967 in a lecture given by Hans Robert Jauss (1921–97), published three years later in the form of a book entitled *Literaturgeschichte als Provokation* (*Literary History as Provocation*), soon followed by two works by Wolfgang Iser: *Der Implizierte Leser* (*The Implied Reader*) (1972) and *Der Akt des Lesens* (*The Act of Reading*) (1976). Jauss founded a new approach called 'the aesthetics of influence and reception'. He contrasted this approach with the aesthetics of production and representation which, in his view, characterised both the traditional Marxist approach and the formalist approach. By 'influence' he meant the text's role in defining reading and consumption by the reader, or receiver, or audience, seen as an indispensable 'partner' of the literary work. By 'reception' he meant the 'successive concretions of a work', the dialogue between the text and the reader which releases, in every historical period, the semantic-artistic potential of the work and places it within the literary tradition. However, readers may also be a factor of conservatism, insofar as their 'horizon of expectations', formed by the literature already produced, offers more or less resistance to the innovative initiatives of the writer.

In *Qu'est-ce que la littérature?* (*What is Literature?*) (1947),

Jean-Paul Sartre had already emphasised the 'joint effort on the part of author and reader in bringing forth the concrete and imaginary object which is a work of the mind'. Researchers who were interested, along with Robert Escarpit, in the problem of literary communication, quoted these reflections of Sartre. In 1958, in a lecture presented at the International Congress of Philosophy which was to provide the basis for the work *The Open Work* (the original Italian version was published in 1962), Umberto Eco linked the question of the co-creative role of the reader and the receiver to the transformation of literature and art, which now seek to produce 'ambiguity as a value', offering works that are manifestly open to a multitude of meanings.

> The artist who produces knows that, through the object, he is structuring a *message*; he cannot ignore the fact that he is working for a *receiver*. He knows that the receiver will interpret the object-message by taking advantage of all its ambiguities, but he does not feel any less responsible as a consequence for this *chain of communication*.

In his essay on the death of the author (1968), Roland Barthes stressed the fact that the ultimate meaning of every cultural text is released by the reader.

Cultural studies and feminist studies

In his preface to David Morley's work *Family Television: Cultural Power and Domestic Leisure* (1986), Stuart Hall wrote:

> The monolithic conception of the viewer, the audience or of television itself have been displaced – one hopes forever – before the new emphasis on difference and variation. It is these variant mappings between these different factors in the social contexts of viewing which Morley has begun to trace. What the mappings reveal, in sum, is the fine-grained interrelationships between meaning, pleasure, use and choice.

The question that had previously preoccupied Hoggart indeed aroused general interest during the 1980s. The receiver was recognised as playing an active role in constructing the meaning of messages and the importance of the context of reception was underscored.

Sociologists belonging to the cultural studies current had already begun tackling this question in important texts published by the Birmingham Centre (see Chapter 4.3). Morley went into greater depth in *Family Television*, which explores family interaction with regard to television within the natural context of television reception, the domestic world. This work brought out the role played by television in the leisure activity of the various family members, what they read, the unequal distribution of decision-making power in choosing programmes, viewing times and different reception behaviours. The ethnographic research for this study was carried out on – and with – eighteen white families living in south London, each composed of two adults and two or more children under eighteen years of age; these families owned a VCR and belonged, for the most part, to the working class or lower middle class. This sample made it possible to observe contrasts between families of different social positions, in terms not only of income but also of cultural capital, as well as between families with children of different ages. Following the US sociologist James Lull, Morley was particularly interested in the question of power relations between the sexes as revealed by television and programme reception.

On this point, his work coincided with the already established current of feminist studies. He openly claimed, moreover, to have found inspiration in the work on women's reading of romance fiction, published between 1983 and 1985 by the American feminist Janice Radway. This current developed out of 'feminist film theory' based on the psychoanalysis and semiotics of cinema. In an article published in the journal *Screen* in 1975, 'Visual Pleasure and Narrative Cinema', British feminist critic Laura Mulvey demonstrated that pleasure is identified in Hollywood films with the masculine point of view and pondered the fact that female spectators were thereby led to share in this pleasure in a masochistic way. While it opened a significant new path for research, this article set off a major controversy within film theory and feminist media studies, with Mulvey herself playing a key role in formulating the arguments. Reflection on the interaction between the text, the context and the female audience quickly focused on the study of television genres specifically aimed at this audience category, with the soap opera naturally standing out as the genre which, since the beginning of the culture industry, had sought and found an audience among female spectators (belonging to certain social strata). These studies showed how the soap opera is composed in such a way as to respond to the expectations of its spectators, by speaking to the responsibilities, tensions and daily routines associated with their position within the couple and the home (M. Mattelart, 1986). This current was well represented within English-speaking countries by such authors as Ann Kaplan (1983) and Tania Modleski (1984) in the United States and Charlotte Brunsdon (1981) in Great Britain, along with Ien Ang (1985) in the Netherlands, among many others.

One of the main theoretical references of this current was the work of American anthropologist Clifford Geertz. In his view, 'Culture is not a power, something to which social events, behaviors, institutions, or processes can be causally attributed. It is a context, something within which they can be intelligibly – that is thickly – described' (Geertz, 1973). As 'interworked systems of construable signs (what, ignoring provincial usages, I would call symbols)', culture is rather 'a complex network of significations' that give a common or public meaning to the behaviours and speech of individual actors. The anthropologist's task is to describe the singularity of the behaviours and speech of these individual actors using what Geertz calls the 'thick description' of social action, which seeks to establish how the actors understand their own behaviour and, on the basis of these conjectures, to state what this reveals about social life. The analysis of systems of symbols is thus not 'an experimental science looking for laws, but an interpretive science looking for meanings', and one must accept the intrinsically fragmentary and incomplete condition of cultural analysis.

'Uses and gratifications'

Functionalist sociology, too, opened up in the 1970s to the ethnographic studies on audience and reception carried out by the so-called 'uses and gratifications' current, which took an interest in 'user satisfaction' by asking the question: What do people do with the media (Blumler and Katz, 1975)? Elihu Katz, one of the leading figures in this sociological current, has explained how it evolved towards this question. The current moved away from theories of direct effects (the behaviourist hypothesis and its variants) and attempted to supersede theories of indirect or limited effects, particularly diffusionist theory and 'agenda-setting studies', according to which the media tell us not what to think but rather what to think about, playing the role of a 'master of ceremonies' or 'bulletin board' where the issues to be debated in society are posted. These theories are known as 'theories of limited effects' because the dictates of an agenda do not prevent networks of interpersonal relations from playing a mediating role. The influence of the media is limited, since the 'selectivity' of receivers acts as an obstacle; it cannot be direct since there are relays; it cannot be immediate, since the process of exerting influence takes time (Katz, 1990).

During the 1980s, the uses and gratifications current developed its own notion of 'negotiated reading': meaning and effects grow out of interaction between texts and the roles assumed by the audience. Decoding is linked to the degree of audience involvement; this involvement depends in turn on the way various cultures construct the role of the receiver. The analysis of the television series *Dallas* provided an opportunity for these hypotheses to be verified. A team directed by Tamar Liebes and Katz, working in connection with the University of Jerusalem, carried out a series of surveys to examine how this programme, which was shown on television worldwide, was received by particular groups in different cultures: Palestinians in Israel, Moroccan Jews, Californians, etc. (Liebes and Katz, 1991).

On the basis of these studies, which restored the activity of the receiver, Katz attempted a convergence between critical theory and functionalist sociology. This convergence may be illustrated by the fact that Morley, by his own affirmation, sought inspiration in certain intuitions of the 'uses and gratifications' school. The fact that both currents treat a subject that had long remained outside the concerns of research was not, however, enough to unite these authors, whose epistemological assumptions sometimes diverged considerably. Moreover, the widespread movement towards the study of the receiver generated a passionate debate which underscored the ambiguities of the enterprise (Dahlgren, 1985; Sfez, 1988; Curran, 1990; Wolf, 1990; Dayan, 1992; Silverstone, 1994).

The consumer and the user: strategic stakes

There was no longer any doubt, however, about the importance of analysing different readings and uses, although it should be specified that this new approach developed in a very particular context which could lead to confusion in interpreting its significance.

Reception and the consumer-individual are central notions in the neo-liberal (i.e., free-market) conception of society. The consumer is not just any consumer, but one who is said to make sovereign choices in a so-called free market – whence the neo-populist drift of some theories of reception. Certain comparative studies on the differing interpretations made by consumers on the basis of their different cultures have helped efface the question of the power of communication, which so obsessed previous generations. In the end, they tacitly lead to the following conclusion: since the power of transmitters of messages is quite relative, contrary to earlier belief, the idea of one transmitter being more powerful than another loses a great deal of its relevance, as does the need for a critical political economy. Indeed, what is the point in dwelling on the unequal exchange of television programmes and films on the international audiovisual market if the power of meaning lies in the hands of the consumer? However simplistic it may seem, this argument has implicitly contributed to invalidating the question of social and economic factors determining individual consumption and the production and consumption of programmes and films in different countries. The stakes attached to manifesting exclusive interest in the question of reception have become clear at a time when the hegemony of US producers is the focal point of discussions in international organisations on free trade and free flow in the audiovisual and telecommunications domains.

More generally, emphasis on the audience's ability to resist may also contribute to minimising the knowledge about consumers' practices that industry requires in order to achieve a redeployment of the social and productive order (M. and A. Mattelart, 1987; Webster and Robins, 1989). Whereas Fordism and Taylorism were based on rationalising the production process through a knowledge of the mechanics of workers' gestures or the kinetics of production, contemporary cybernetic rationality requires knowledge to manage not just production, but consumption as well. The consumer, once *terra incognita*, indeed becomes both the subject and object of research, as demonstrated by the sharp rise in the use of techniques to measure consumer 'targets' and life styles – techniques that are constantly refined through computerised production technologies and the storage of data on individuals and groups. The action informed by knowledge exercised on consumers attempts to decompose their movements and sound out their needs and desires. The knowledge of these movements and desires informs and feeds the circular movement of programming, production and consumption, which, though always unstable, tends none the less towards the functional and affective integration of the consumer into the mechanisms of the market economy.

This is what some sociologists have apparently failed to see, in their jubilation at the collapse of the postulates of a sociology of power and social reproduction. 'Programs are produced, distributed and defined by the industry; texts are the products of their readers' (Fiske, 1987).

French researchers, unlike their counterparts in English-speaking countries, have preferred to emphasise the mechanisms of socialisation of communicating devices. (This attitude may have been encouraged by the success of the Minitel.) They have striven to build a socio-political approach to the uses of new information and communication technologies. Some authors have underlined the importance of mediation and interaction in the collective construction of technical objects and shown that the formation of the social use of these techniques involves complex processes of combining technical and social innovation (Boullier, 1984; Laulan, 1986; Jouët, 1987, 1993; Perriault, 1989; Flichy, 1991; Moeglin, 1991, 1994; Vedel, 1994; Vitalis, 1994).

Michel de Certeau (1926–86) opened the way to theoretical discussion of the uses and 'practices' of users in a book entitled

L'Invention du quotidien. Arts de faire (*The Practice of Everyday Life*) (1980). He stressed the ability of users to subvert or 'circumnavigate' the rational mechanisms set up by the state and market order. In counterpoint to Michel Foucault's analyses of 'networks of observational and disciplinary technology', Certeau considered it indispensable to explore the 'networks of anti-discipline'. His work has been widely quoted in studies on reception and mediation all over the world and has sometimes been used to justify the idea that since power can be averted by the many procedures of consumption, it no longer exists. Yet Michel de Certeau's analyses were driven by the intimate conviction that the mechanisms of subjection are ever-present. He was anxious to specify the nature of user 'tactics' or 'operations' since *power relations* define the networks in which such tactics come into play and delimit the circumstances in which they can be successfully applied: 'It is a matter of combat and play between the strong and the weak, and of the actions still possible for the weak' (Certeau, 1980).

Michel de Certeau: the culture of consumption

The analysis of images distributed by television, the amount of time spent in front of the set, the choices made by users, etc. do not yet tell us anything about what the consumer *does* during this time and with these images. Yet there lies the real question: how do users *produce* their practices in the imposed spaces of the city, the supermarket, the media, the office, etc.? We know less and less about this as the totalitarian extension of production systems increasingly leaves consumers without a place to record what they do with products, and the scientific apparatus, participating in the logic of these systems, measures the progress of these products in economic networks but remains blind to their actual use by the consumer. To production that has been rationalised and expansionist as well as centralised, noisy and spectacular, there corresponds another kind of production (known as 'consumption'), which is clever, dispersed while insinuating itself everywhere, silent and virtually invisible, since it is not does call attention to itself through the products themselves but through the ways of using them imposed by a dominant economic order. (Interview in *Le Monde*, 31 January 1978.)

7 *The Dominion of Communication*

Sociological theory's return to the study of social bonds built through everyday communication came at a time when complex technological systems of communication and information were playing a structuring role in organising society and transforming the world order.

Society was defined in terms of communication, which in turn was defined in terms of networks. Cybernetics had displaced the mathematical theory of information.

1 The notion of the network

The critique of diffusionism

During the 1960s, Everett Rogers had restricted the definition of innovation to that which is 'communicated through certain channels over time among the members of a social system'. Innovation consisted in transmitting data of whose usefulness future users would still have to be persuaded. The model was in keeping with the one-dimensional conception of progress which held that modernisation and the adoption of innovations necessarily brought about 'development'. According to this view, any refusal had to be due to persistent features of so-called traditional cultures. In practice, diffusionist strategy came down to product marketing (see Chapter 2.2).

Some twenty years later, Rogers revisited his theory critically. Judging it too closely linked to mathematical information theory, he criticised it for its tendency to neglect context, to define interlocutors as isolated atoms, and, above all, to rely on one-way mechanical causality. He proposed to replace it with a definition of communication as a 'convergence process in which the participants create and share information with one another in order to reach mutual understanding' (Rogers and Kincaid, 1981). In place of the former diffusionist model, he proposed 'communication network analysis'. A network is composed of individuals connected to one another by patterned communications flows.

The analysis of *communication structure* (or network) as the arrangement of the differentiated elements of a system requires defining the main subsystems. This model implied new research procedures consisting in (1) identifying *cliques*, defined as a subsystem whose elements interact with each other relatively more frequently than with other members of the communication system; (2) identifying certain specialised communication roles such as *liaisons* (an individual linking two or more cliques in a system, but who is not affiliated to any clique), *bridges* (an individual linking two or more cliques from his position as a member of one of the cliques) and *isolates*; and (3) measuring communication structural indexes (such as communication connectedness) for individuals, dyads, personal networks, cliques or entire systems.

The model was restricted to the question of adopting innovations; it was given legitimacy by references to Gregory Bateson's ecology of mind, Georg Simmel's ideas on the web of group-affiliations and the sociometry of Jacob L. Moreno (1892–1974). The last was a social psychologist of Romanian origin who settled in the United States, where he developed a methodological basis for measuring the different variables in a 'network' of relations and quantifying the models of communication between individuals within a system. This schema or 'sociogramme' indicated the positive and negative attitudes of the members of a group and designated key individuals and leaders. For Moreno, it constituted an essential step in the search for 'harmonic community' (Moreno, 1934). The emerging development of light communication technologies (video, micro-computers) appeared to favour the advent of the horizontal model that Rogers counterposed to the heavy apparatus of centralised media systems on which diffusionism had based its vertical schema of persuasion.

By 1982, Rogers had concluded that the necessary conditions were present to undertake a reconciliation of 'critical research' with what he called 'empirical research', thereby setting off a controversy within critical research circles in the United States. Rogers justified this reconciliation, which would have been unthinkable a few years earlier, by the fact that the empirical school had realised the need to include in its analysis the question of the communication context, the ethical aspects of the communication process and a plurality of methods. Rogers' proposal was interpreted not as a possible opening to dialogue but rather as an expression of the will to deny epistemological differences and to dodge an essential point related to the definition of the political: the conditions required for the exercise of power, the relationship between power and knowledge, and the role of organisational and institutional structures (Slack and Allor, 1983).

Rogers's desire to bring about the convergence of empirical and critical research – shared by Katz – indicated a new state of mind.

The notion of a network served to mask society's profoundly segregated condition, offering a harmonious vision in its place. At a time when various forms of exclusion were becoming blatantly manifest, 'the ideology of communication, the new egalitarianism through communication, [was] fulfilling its legitimising function' (A. and M. Mattelart, 1986).

In the 1980s, Bruno Latour and Michel Callon, two sociologists at the Centre for Sociology and Innovation at the École des Mines in Paris, developed an anthropology of science and technology which also placed the notion of network at the heart of their conceptual framework by rejecting the diffusionist model in favour of a model of 'translation' or socio-technological construction (Callon, 1986; Latour, 1987). Refusing to take technology and science as given, they sought to grasp them in action and to study how they constitute themselves. In their view, they deploy a two-fold set of strategies or a deployment of forces, that is, a strategy for mobilising human actors and enlisting non-human elements (e.g., wind, sand, concrete, ocean currents, shellfish larvae). 'Translating' meant putting these heterogeneous elements into a network or system of mutual dependence. Innovators must find allies, become spokesmen and develop tactics that appeal to individual interest in order to lead their interlocutors – both human and non-human – into new networks or sets of alliances. That is how a particular scientific statement is made credible.

Their approach refused the possibility of a 'pure' social sphere limited to relations between human beings; they postulated the interpenetration of human relationships with nature and technological objects. Social bonds were thus introduced into machines.

While there was general agreement on the heuristic value of the 'translation' model, it was criticised by some sociologists of communication on two counts. Louis Quéré objected that there was a danger of overestimating the freedom of manoeuvre of the actor and the actor-network by obliterating the normative dimensions of the social bond, that is, the idea that the social bond cannot be established on random foundations or by chance. The second objection, directed at the model's conception of technology, drew attention to the constraints inherent in technological objects themselves and their internal logics. Louis Quéré expressed these as follows, drawing inspiration from another theoretician of technology, Georges Simondon: 'By rejecting the idea of an essence of technology, we also run the risk of excluding the very principle of the operational functioning of machines, which involves a succession of ordered rather than haphazard or arbitrary mediations' (Quéré, 1989; Simondon, 1969).

The cognitive sciences

'Understanding the act of knowing' is the aim of the cognitive sciences. Their field is 'cognition', that is, knowledge as an activity rather than as a state or a content. They study the processes whereby knowledge is formed, processes which may be encountered both in the world of living organisms and in 'intelligent' machines. The emergence of these sciences cannot be separated from cognitive technology, from the 'thinking machines' that reproduce mental activities such as comprehension, perception and decision-making. These sciences do not make up a unified body of knowledge but rather constitute a broad intersection of disciplines as diverse as neurology, biology, psychology, linguistics and anthropology; within each of these coexist approaches that may not always be compatible.

The cognitive sciences were born in the 1940s in the United States along with the cybernetic movement and at the same time as information theory and the rising use of mathematical logic to describe the workings of the nervous system and the human reasoning process. They further developed during the second half of the 1950s with the 'cognitivist hypothesis', according to which intelligence, including human intelligence, is so similar to that of a computer that cognition can be defined as *computation* of symbolic representations, while symbols are defined as 'items representing that to which they correspond'. Artificial intelligence was a literal projection of this theory. The notion of *representation* lies at the core of cognitive theory. It leads to interpreting the workings of the brain as a data processing system which reacts selectively to the environment or to information coming from the outside world. Artificial intelligence conceives of organisation as an open system of inputs and outputs, in constant interaction with this environment.

Two Chilean biologists, Humberto Maturana and Francisco J. Varela, refuted this conception of the open system by developing the idea of *autopoiesis* and the autopoietic system (from the Greek *autos*, self, and *poiein*, produce).

> An autopoietic system is organised like a network of processes to produce components that (a) continually regenerate, through their transformations and interactions, the network that produced them, and (b) constitute the system as a concrete unit in the space in which it exists, by specifying the topological domain in which it produces itself as a network. (Maturana and Varela, 1980)

Autopoietic organisation implies autonomy, circularity and self-reference.

> An autopoietic machine continually engenders and specifies its own organisation. It accomplishes a ceaseless process of replacing its components because it is continually subject to outside disturbances and is constantly forced to compensate for them. Thus, an autopoietic machine is a homeostatic system (or better yet, a system of stable relations) whose basic invariant is its own organisation (the network of relations that defines it). (Varela, 1989)

The notion of representation was the main target of the critique: according to the representationist school, a cognitive entity always refers to a pre-existing world. Information, in the autopoietic approach, however, is not pre-established as an intrinsic order, but is an emerging order of cognitive activities themselves. The distinctive feature of our everyday cognitive activity is the act of 'bringing forth', which creates a world. 'Cognition is the combined advent of a world and a mind starting from the history of the various actions that a creature accomplishes in the world' (Varela, 1989). The term chosen by the two biologists to designate this operation is *enaction*.

Whereas the cognitive sciences were developed on the east coast of the United States, particularly at MIT, the theory of autopoiesis and enaction aimed at breaking with Western science, which was seen as cut off from human experience and with the way individuals perceive things. The theory of autopoeisis and enaction is interested, on the contrary, in the 'embodiment of the mind', as expressed by the title of one of Varela's books (1993) written in collaboration with Evan Thompson and Eleanor Rosch. It has developed a dialogue with Buddhist meditative psychology and claims filiation with the phenomenological tradition (that of Husserl but, above all, Merleau-Ponty) and the critique of representation carried out by Foucault – all thinkers who, in their words, 'were concerned about the phenomenon of *interpretation* as a whole, in its circular meaning of a link between action and knowledge, between the knower and the known'. This circular relationship between action and interpretation is what the expression 'bringing forth' seeks to convey.

Although it represents a minority within the mosaic of cognitive sciences, the autopoietic approach attempts to describe the co-emergence of the individual and social worlds. It can be credited with reminding us that the cognitive abilities of an individual are linked not only to the brain but also to the body, in contrast with other sectors of the cognitive sciences that reduce human intelligence to a mechanical system. There is a danger that the penchant for totalising conceptualisations, characteristic of these sectors, may lead them very far towards biological interpretations of the world and confirm their complicity in bringing back Social Darwinist theories that thrive in the atmosphere of neo-liberalism. Therein lie the contradictory challenges that the sciences of living organisms present to the social sciences of communication.

2 One world, many societies

Globalisation and its ambiguities

Interpretive sociology was not the only discipline to be caught up in the tension between micro and macro levels. Such tension was also at work in the political economy of communication, in the critical investigations of the complex bonds uniting particular territories to the world sphere in the age of cross-border networks. To account more fully for this phenomenon, new interdisciplinary combinations were created, involving history, geography, geopolitics, political science, industrial economy and anthropology.

All these intersecting views, which were part of a broader process of a shifting of the frontiers separating disciplines, stimulated researchers in the political economy of communication to engage in a critical reassessment of their academic territory. At the same time, this epistemological rethinking process led them, in the second half of the 1980s, to take a stand against the fundamental ambiguity characterising the evolution of an important sector of cultural studies (see the controversy between Nicholas Garnham, 1995, and Larry Grossberg, 1995). In keeping with the objections put forth by geographers, historians and political scientists, political economists of communication thus criticised several trends in contemporary cultural studies: their tendency to yield to 'receptionitis', that is, to reduce all the interesting questions involving the media to one dimension, and thereby revive a certain 'media-centrism'; a relationship to field work which, when undertaken, was all too often limited to the home or the shopping mall, sites for the reception of programmes or the consumption of commodities; the failure to take into account the economic and historical dimensions; an a-critical rallying to the notion of 'globalisation', in which power is defined once and for all as 'scattered, diffuse, dissipated, volatile, complex, interactive' and therefore an 'elusive' and irrelevant object of research, with the significant result of eroding the notion of 'resistance'; finally, and more generally, the inflation of meta-discourse on complexity at the expense of the search for a theory of complexity – in short, an apparent conceptual sophistication which masked a highly conformist type of thinking, ill at ease in the face of the multidimensional character of the new intercultural balance of forces in the context of spreading technology and production systems (A. and M. Mattelart, 1986; Golding and Murdock, 1991; McGuigan, 1992; Gregory, 1993; Morley and Robins, 1995; A. Mattelart and Neveu, 1996; Mosco, 1996; D. Schiller, 1996; Roach, 1997). It is often impossible to engage a genuine controversy between cultural studies and political economy. Many sociologists, to avoid it, fail to recognise any contribution of political economy of communication and culture after the 1970s, thereby freezing and devaluing it (Tomlinson, 1991; J.B. Thompson, 1995). Evidence of this kind of extreme simplification can be found in the ritual, rather outmoded debates in the 1990s on 'cultural imperialism'. Lacking even the most elementary epistemological precaution and sometimes actually bordering on intellectual dishonesty, these debates have taken the notion out of context, abstracting it from the concrete historical conditions that produced it: the political struggles and commitments of the 1960s and 1970s. The most relevant criticism of the notion is certainly not to be found in these belated denunciations, which are merely a-historical caricatures, but rather in the dynamics of self-criticism in the field of political economy itself, in its endeavour to rethink its territory so as to make culture's new position in the reorganised world order politically intelligible.

The various disciplinary fields in the human and social sciences have contributed in very different measures to the renewal of research on the relations among local, national and worldwide levels, since they did not all feel the same need to create alliances in order to study the new importance of communication networks. Internationalisation is no longer what it was when the concepts of dependency and cultural imperialism could still be used to apprehend the imbalance in worldwide flows of information and communication, because new actors have appeared on what is now a trans-national scene. States and inter-state relations are no longer the sole mainspring of world organisation. The major information and communication networks, with their 'invisible', 'immaterial' flows, form 'abstract territories' that no longer correspond to old notions of territoriality. By attacking the institutional foundations of nation-states in the 1980s, the logics of construction of the techno-financial macrosystem modified the topology of the actors of the trans-national sphere. The end of the bi-polar tension between superpowers enhanced the role of market relations in the configuration of the world space. The incorporation of the territories of nation-states into the norms of planetary networks augurs a profound transformation of the economic and social model, that is, the organisational forms of overall social relations within each society.

The designers of new 'global' or multinational firms, the 'organic intellectuals' of management thinking, have also experienced the tension between micro and macro. Transformed into producers of theories and doctrines, they have brought confusion to the conceptual field of communication in the age of globalisation (this latter term itself being a perfect example of how notions can become loaded).

The notion of globalisation, derived from a management conception of worldwide economic organisation, came into widespread use just as communication networks began to be deregulated and privatised. The process began with the deregulation of banking activities in the United States during the 1970s, but it was not fully deployed until 1984, with the dismantling of the American Telegraph and Telephone Company, which had previously enjoyed a virtual private monopoly on telecommunications. Since then, the term has increasingly come into use all over the world in highly varied sectors of economic activity. Deregulation means that the centre of gravity of society shifts to the market, which becomes the principal factor of a new type of regulation. As corporate values and private interests became predominant, a process that coincided with the shrinking of public service and the welfare state and the decline of social forces supporting them, communication activity changed its nature and status: it became professionalised, fuelling many new fields of competence and many new lines of business. The entrepreneurial model of communication was promoted as a technology for managing social relationships and imposed recognition as the only effective method for establishing links with the various components of society. This management approach was tested in the marketplace and became the sole reference in matters of communication strategy for state institutions, humanitarian associations and local and regional governments.

At the end of the 1980s, the decade of deregulation, the idea of globalisation and universal standardisation was combined with the theory of the 'end of history', formulated by Francis Fukuyama (1992), though it was already present in Zbigniew Brzezinski's analyses of 'global society' (see Chapter 5.2). The early notion of globalisation conveys a conception of world order based on the principles of the only system that survived the Cold War, the capitalist regime of commodity production. The name of this system is now passed over in silence because, once the Berlin Wall had collapsed, it became naturalised as the only possible mode of living, culture, development and democracy. The networks of this system are dominated by large corporations, and despite their claims to have become civic actors, as they have proclaimed in image-building campaigns, it cannot be forgotten that they are based on the search for profit and exclusive interest in solvent sectors of society.

A hybrid planet

Critical thought rejects this new totalising idea according to which humanity has reached a stage which cannot be surpassed. Some authors, who take as an assumption that the notions of 'globality' and the world sphere are social constructions, have tried to reconnect them to history and show how they are components of 'integrated world capitalism' (Guattari, 1987). They have placed the economy of immaterial flows in the context of their material origins. The concept of 'world-communication', inspired by that of 'world-economy', serves to pursue the analysis of this new, hierarchically organised, trans-national sphere in which the logic of large networks generates a dynamic of integration while at the same time producing new forms of segregation, exclusion and disparity (A. Mattelart, 1992, 1994). The 'world-system' is organised in a 'Hanseatic' mode, that is, around a few points which draw the main flows of the globalised economy. These include mega-cities or mega-regions, usually in the North, sometimes in the South, and the three poles of 'triadic power', to use the expression of Kenichi Ohmae (1985), a Japanese theoretician of cross-border management: the European Union, North America and Eastern Asia. The 'globalised' world is the global marketplace; it is defined in terms of the flows branching out from the centres of market power. Despite their own social imbalances, the main industrial countries are still the sole reference. Diffusionist theory, rejected by micro-sociologies that can be naive in the face of such questions of balance of forces, has surreptitiously made its return.

The 1970s were marked by the study of the logics of de-territorialisation and emphasised the strategies of macro-subjects (nation-states, major international organisations, multinational firms). During the following decades, researchers paid more attention to the logics of re-territorialisation and the mediating and negotiating processes at work between external constraints and localised realities. The questioning of the essentialist conception of 'universality' and the Western 'logos' encouraged other actors to produce new concepts and theories, for example the anthropological research on trans-national cultures and identities in the face of the flows of global modernity and its ethnoscapes, technoscapes, finance-scapes, mediascapes and ideoscapes, to use the terms of Arjun Appadurai. In Asia as well Latin America, such research has examined the complex processes of appropriation and re-appropriation, resistance and mimetism. New concepts arose, such as *créolisation*, *métissage*, hybridisation and alternative modernity, expressing a desire to understand more fully these articulations (Martín Barbero, 1987; Ortiz, 1988; Apparadurai, 1990; García Canclini, 1990). The same desire has inspired research on the genealogy of the genres of local audiovisual industries that draw wide audiences in particular territories (Sarló, 1985; Allen, 1985,

1995; M. and A. Mattelart, 1987; Martín Barbero and Muñoz, 1992; Ortiz et al., 1989; Mazziotti, 1996).

In Latin America, these analyses have given rise to original investigations into the articulation between popular cultures and industrial cultural production. At the same time, studies on reception by the popular sectors of the *telenovela* – the Latin-American television genre *par excellence* – have generated growing interest among researchers in this region. Efforts are being made to put the science of social and cultural practices to work in developing 'active' teaching methods supported by mass television programmes as the vector of knowledge (Martín Barbero, 1987; Fuenzalida and Hermosilla, 1991; CENECA, 1992; Orozco Gómez, 1996a and 1996b).

The expansion of the forms of communication used by non-governmental organisations or other associations of civil society constitutes another unprecedented aspect of the process of globalisation. These new social networks are now taken into account in the debate on the possibility of a public sphere at the planetary level. All over the world, the transformation in the public sphere – both national and international – has become an important issue in critical approaches inspired by sociology, political science and political economy (Quéré, 1982; Garnham, 1990; Keane, 1990; Miège, 1989a, 1990; H. Schiller, 1989; Schlesinger, 1991; Raboy and Dagenais, 1992; Neveu, 1994; Grewal and Kaplan, 1994).

All this is taking place in a context in which the terms of the question of the imbalance of information flows have changed so radically that some have denied any such imbalance. These discussions are now held within organisations like GATT (transformed in 1995 into the World Trade Organisation, WTO), where the debate on cultural products has been incorporated into that concerning free exchange of services, thereby giving renewed legitimacy to the neo-liberal thesis on the free flow of information.

An unbridled global market has created tension between 'freedom of commercial speech' and citizens' freedom of speech. The government authorities that were demanding the creation of a new world order of information and communication in the 1970s are gone, while in the most privileged countries of the now fragmented third world, a new development objective has been put forward: hitching their wagon to the first world. 'Yankee go home! But take us with you!' says a slogan painted on walls from Port-au-Prince to Tijuana.

How have the countless branches of the networks making up the web of globalisation acquired a meaning for each community and culture? How have they resisted, adapted or yielded? Tensions and gaps among the plurality of cultures, and the centrifugal forces of mercantile cosmopolitanism reveal the complexity of reactions to the emerging single global market.

Even as we point out the potential benefits of examining the interaction and fragmentation in the global market, we must hasten to stress the ambivalence of this approach. It may encourage critical questioning of the relationship between unifying logics and the organisation of democratic life on a daily basis, but it can also conciliate itself with multiple forms of withdrawal into cultural or ethnic identity.

Towards a new status of knowledge

'Our societies are moving into the post-industrial age and our cultures into the post-modern age,' wrote the French philosopher Jean-François Lyotard in *La Condition postmoderne* (*The Postmodern Condition*) in 1979. In Lyotard's judgement, the basis of the principle of social division – class struggle – has become so blurred as to lose all radicality. From this he deduced the demise of the credibility of grand narratives and their decomposition.

The narrative function is losing its functioners: the great heroes, the great perils, the great voyages, the great goal. The novelty is that in this context, the former poles of attraction constituted by nation-states, parties, professions, institutions and historical traditions are losing their appeal. And it does not seem that they are likely to be replaced, at least not on the same scale [. . .]. 'Identifications' with great names, with heroes of present history, are becoming more difficult.

The idea of post-modernity has been at work in architecture, aesthetics, literature and sociology since the early 1960s. In political sociology, the road to the concept of 'post-industrial society' was paved largely by distinctly partisan theories such as the theory of the end of ideology (see Chapter 2.2).

Following the example of Daniel Bell, sociologists thought the post-modern age could be dated from the rise of information machines, but some theoreticians of aesthetics have been more cautious, hoping thereby to avoid the traps of technological determinism in the so-called post-industrial age. For example, in Umberto Eco's opinion, it is difficult to determine the rise of the post-modern current chronologically and he interprets it as a 'spiritual category, or better still a *Kunstwollen*, a way of operating. We could say that every period has its own post-modernism' (Eco, 1982). The American critic Frederic Jameson, on the other hand, has proposed to locate post-modernism as a well-defined historical stage in the evolution of regimes of thought, analysing it as a break from modernist thought. Post-modernism, as the dominant cultural feature of the logic of late capitalism, is characterised by the critique of 'depth models': the dialectical model of essence and appearance, with its concepts of ideology and false consciousness; the existential model of authenticity or lack of authenticity with its founding opposition between alienation and disalienation. Finally, there is the great semiotic opposition between signifier and signified that prevailed during the 1960s and 1970s.

Global market and local realities

The term 'globalisation' came into widespread use in the 1980s as a result of changes in the world economy and its emerging technological networks for real-time data transmission. It grew out of the notion of 'financial globalisation' or the strategic restructuring of the international financial sphere, which sanctioned the de-linking of capital markets rather from nation-states and the increased dependence of national systems of production with respect to the world market. Indeed, despite signs of chronic instability, it was in this sector of economic activity that the greatest advances in building a planetary sphere took place. The 'financialisation' of the economy in a sense reflected the entire decade: speculative movements were intensified and the risk of volatility increased, with market crashes sending shock waves all across the electronically connected world. Stock exchanges and the great speculative fevers, which Robert E. Park had already seen in the 1920s as metaphor of the world of the news, confirmed their role as a portent of upheavals affecting the circuits of information exchange.

The notion of globalisation was extended from networks of financial flows to networks of economic and cultural flows, through the efforts of management and marketing theoreticians. The first to use it in this sense was Theodor Levitt, who published an article entitled 'The Globalization of Markets' in 1983 in the *Harvard Business Review*, of which he was then editor. Levitt maintained that increasingly uniformised needs result in increasing uniformisation of the market and approach to customers. The rise of competition on a global scale requires a global strategic vision of market planning. A powerful force is leading the world towards what Levitt called 'a converging commonality': technology. The process of corporate concentration and the establishment of multimedia and advertising mega-groups now under way only confirms the hypothesis of 'universal standardisation' of which they are the new economic agents. Consequently, the only form of organisation capable of 'decimating competitors' in the hyper-competitive market is the 'global firm', which operates as if the entire world were a single unit and thinks of its products, services, distribution and communication in 'global terms'. According to this global or 'holistic' mode of thinking, which recycles analogies of the living organism, a company is a dynamic whole, a 'system' whose 'globalisation' is both internal and external. It is internal in the sense that global firms claim to put an end to the rigid hierarchies and pyramidal forms of authority inherited from the Fordist and Taylorist models of organisation in which holding back information was a source of knowledge and power. Instead, they adopt a 'communicational' or network-based model of management determined by the need for the free flow of ideas on design, production, distribution, synergy of skills, transfer of know-how and interaction in work organisation. Globalisation is also external in that global firms represent a mode of relationship to the world market. Globalisation thus becomes a cybernetic grid for viewing the world and an embryonic new world order. Not all of these theorists took such extreme positions; some of them pointed out that market segmentation and targeting were just as important as standardisation.

Beyond these differences, from the standpoint of this management theory of the world market, globalisation means that the conception of space as divided into self-contained layers or levels had become as obsolete as the compartmentalised organisation of work. Under the previous management system, local, national and international levels were represented as mutually impervious stages. The new schema for representing the company and the world in which it operates as a production and distribution network involves a model of interaction among all three levels. All strategy in a globalised market has to be at once local and international, a notion expressed by Japanese management theorists through the term 'glocalize', a neologism that has appeared in the *Oxford Dictionary of New Words* since 1991. The logic of the so-called global firm is governed by a single watchword: the 'integration' of the different geographical scales alongside that of research and design, production and marketing (hence the new role of 'co-producer' attributed to the consumer or user).

The project of integrating the global firm cannot be separated from the creation of a 'corporate culture' consisting of shared values, beliefs, rituals and objectives, one of whose goals is indeed to forge an alliance between the local and global levels. Corporate culture cannot be located in a particular territory. It is rather a mindset which allows global identity to avoid being overrun by different identities based on belonging to a national or local territory. Other theorists of the return to corporate culture, however, temper this postulate with another: the need for 'cross-cultural management', which consists in mixing together and cross-fertilising company management practices rooted in definite histories and cultures, in which the 'modern' and the 'traditional', national '*habitus*' and trans-national patterns all overlap (Iribarne, 1989; Drucker, 1993; Gay, 1997).

In its place, we have been presented with a 'surface model', or rather a model of multiple surfaces. The world, Jameson noted, is losing its depth and threatens to become a shiny surface, a stereo-scopic illusion, a flow of filmic images lacking in density (Jameson, 1984). Celebrating the apotheosis of space in relation to time, and the disappearance of historical reference, the surface model is in phase with the new breadth of the global expansion of trans-national capitalism, its real-time circulation in office information system networks and the flow of universal yet fragmented images.

Lyotard's text was written for a particular occasion: it was a report on the state of knowledge in the most highly developed societies, written at the request of the Québec government's University Council. It aimed at contributing to the widespread debate in the major industrial countries at the time on the question of legitimacy, in a context marked by increasing use of information devices and the 'hegemony of information technology'; a crisis in metaphysics and the discourses of truth; the rise of operational or technological criteria that make it impossible to decide what is true or just; a crisis affecting the great theoretical systems and the triumph of language-game pragmatics.

Harold Innis, a precursor of McLuhan

Harold Adams Innis (1894–1952), a Canadian geographer and political economist, held that communications technology was the basis of political and economic processes. It was only towards the end of his life, however, that Innis actually formulated this hypothesis and began testing it (after several monographic stud-ies on fisheries, the fur trade and railways). Two works attest to his belated interest: *Empire and Communications* (1950) and *The Bias of Communication* (1951).

The theme of the 'empire' refers to the two-fold domination – US and British – to which Canada is exposed. Innis attempted to analyse the difference between them. He wrote his book at a time when the threat from the technological communications system of Canada's powerful neighbours, capable of striking at the 'heart of cultural life in Canada' and provoking a crisis, was becoming clear. The 'biases' of communication in its different technological aspects determine the form of social organisation. Technologically determined 'knowledge monopolies' control the distribution of political power among social groups. Power involves the control of space and time. Communication systems shape social organisation because they structure temporal and spatial relations. Historically, there have been two kinds of media or communication, which have given rise to two different kinds of empires. The first one, which is 'space-binding' (a space bias), is symbolised by the printing press and electronic communication and leads to expansion and to the control of a territory. The second, which is 'time-binding' (a time bias), is sustained by oral culture and manuscripts and fosters memory, a sense of history, small communities and traditional forms of power. The first aims at centralising; the second, at de-centralising. The development of a monopoly on knowledge linked to time and space is the basis of absolute power and represents a serious threat. In Innis's view, Canada was in the unusual position of being sandwiched between two empires, at the very point where the two biases of commu-nication came together. It has been forced to combine opposing technological forces. To combat the effects of technological deter-minism, which restricts the range of possible responses and discussion on the part of audiences, it is necessary to re-establish the 'oral tradition', revive memory and create channels of demo-cratic participation, all elements that form the basis of an alternative kind of communication.

Marshall McLuhan (1911–80), a colleague of Innis at the University of Toronto, acknowledged his debt in *The Gutenberg*

Galaxy (1962): 'Harold Innis was the first person to hit upon the process of change as implicit in the forms of media technology. The present book is a footnote of explanation to his work.'

In this work, Lyotard raised a question that was to be increasingly debated, namely, the status of knowledge and the processes affecting our ways of thinking, teaching and processing information in the era of digital signs and the new alliance of sound, image and text. One author whose work attests to the importance of these questions is Pierre Lévy, who, banking on the emergence of new ways of writing determined by 'digital plasticity', has placed his hopes in the advent of 'collective intelligence', thanks to the 'information highways' of the post-media era that provide a basis for the ultimate communication utopia: 'real-time democracy' (Lévy, 1990, 1994). Other thinkers with more critical distance have attempted to conceive a new political economy of intelligence, reflecting on the consequences of the growing ties between new information and communication technologies and new intellectual technologies, for example in the field of work training and organisation (Girsic, 1994).

Régis Debray's ambitious project of laying the foundations of a 'general mediology', heralded in his book *Le Pouvoir intellectuel en France* (1979), has taken shape progressively. His analysis of the intellectual's 'transmitting' function – the high priest officiating at the controls of transmitting apparatuses – provided the point of departure for his 'mediological' approach, which seeks to establish the 'systematic correlation between symbolic activities such as ideology, politics and culture, on the one hand, and forms of organisation, systems of authority engendered by different modes of production, classification and transmission, on the other hand'. Debray has borrowed from the ideas of Marshall McLuhan, who contributed significantly to demolishing the postulate of the priority of content over form, inherited from the culture of 'typographical man', insisting on the fact that the medium itself determines the nature of what is communicated and leads to a new type of civilisation. In its effort to avoid glorifying technological determinism, mediology seeks above all to reveal 'the objective determinations of the apparatuses of thought' (Debray, 1991). In his studies on technology and memory, Bernard Stiegler has adopted a similar philosophical approach (Stiegler, 1994).

As early as 1977, in *The Domestication of the Savage Mind*, the British anthropologist Jack Goody had developed his seminal ideas on the manner in which different modes of reasoning and perceiving were engendered by different channels of transmission.

The new technological environment forces us to consider the role of the machine in producing subjectivity, a question that preoccupied the French psychoanalyst, Félix Guattari, until his death in 1992. Guattari thought that technological information and communication devices – from data processing to robotics and the media – act upon 'the core of human subjectivity, not only in its memories and its intelligence, but also in its sensitivity, its emotions and its unconscious'. Rejecting post-modern ideology, which he saw as the 'paradigm of all forms of submission and compromise with the status quo', he fought for reappropriation and re-individualisation of the use of communication devices, with a view to social experimentation and the 'constitution of complexes of subjectivation: a plurality of individual–group–machine-exchanges' (Guattari, 1992).

They don't rock the boat, they're just trendy

The post-modernists have hardly innovated at all. They are simply following in the footsteps of structuralism – a very modernist tradition indeed – whose influence in the human sciences seems to have been carried forward under the worst conditions by Anglo-Saxon systems theory. The secret link between all these doctrines has to do with their being subterranean, marked by reductionist conceptions that characterised information theory and early cybernetic research in the immediate post-war period. The references various authors were incessantly deriving from new communication and computer technologies were so hasty, so poorly mastered, that they set us back, far behind the phenomenological research that had come before.

We must go back to an idea that is both simple and obvious yet laden with consequences, namely that concrete social orderings – which should not be confused with the 'primary groups' of sociology in the United States, for they still refer only to an economy of opinion – bring into play many things besides linguistic performance. [They also involve] ethological and ecological dimensions, semiotic, economic, aesthetic, corporeal and phantasmagorical components, irreducible to the semiotics of language, and a multitude of incorporeal worlds of reference that do not easily fit into the coordinates of dominant empirical science.

The post-modern philosophers may flit around pragmatic research as much as they like; they have remained faithful to a structuralist conception of speech and language that will never allow them to connect subjective facts to the formation of the unconscious and aesthetic and micro-political perspectives. To put it plainly, post-modernism is not a philosophy, it is an ambient state of mind, a 'condition' of opinion that draws its truths only from the atmosphere of the times. Why, for example, should it take the trouble to elaborate a serious speculative demonstration of its thesis regarding the thin consistency of the *socius*?

(F. Guattari, 'L'impasse post-moderne', *La Quinzaine littéraire*, 15 February 1986.)

It is precisely the possibility of using communication technology for 'decent purposes' that has been contested by thinkers such as Paul Virilio, Gianni Vattimo and Jean Baudrillard. Virilio's writings, which privilege the use of quotations and aphorisms, demonstrate his scepticism regarding the very possibility of a theory of technology. The accelerating changes that technology is undergoing provide the grounds for his thought, which he places under the sign of 'dromology' (from a Greek word suggesting speed). This acceleration is inversely proportionate to inertia, which forms the horizon of human activity. What until now had appeared as the sign of a handicap or infirmity (the inability to move in order to act) becomes a symbol of progress and command of the environment. Confinement to the home and the possibility of doing everything through a complex of screens are the other side of the search for ubiquity, immediacy and hyper-perception. What is lost is the sense of duration, the movement of the body along with social life. 'When there is no longer time to share,' he writes, 'democracy is no longer possible' (Virilio, 1990).

Enlightenment belief in social progress and individual emancipation was accompanied by notions of communication and transparency. These ideas have become suspect today: communication has become the victim of too much communication (Baudrillard). This excess of communication has produced an implosion of meaning, the loss of a sense of reality and the reign of simulacra. For the Italian philosopher Gianni Vattimo, media society is far from being a 'more enlightened, better educated and more self-aware' society. On the contrary, it is more complex, even chaotic, and 'our hope of emancipation lies in this relative "chaos"'. There is no more History, no more Reality, no more Truth. The world of communication has exploded under the pressure of a multiplicity of local, ethnic, sexual and religious rationalities. This liberation of diversities may offer the 'chance for a new way of (finally?) being human.' Media society replaces 'an emancipating ideal modelled on fulfilled self-awareness, on the perfect discernment of the human being who knows the way things happen' with 'an ideal of emancipation based rather on oscillation, plurality and ultimately, on the erosion of the "reality principle" itself' (Vattimo, 1989).

Baudrillard does not share Vattimo's relative optimism. He has detected in the escalation of technology and its increasing sophistication at the planetary level as well as in the private sphere the advance of a system of control that is buoyed by our 'fantasy of communication': the widespread compulsion to exist on every screen and at the core of every program. 'Am I a man, am I a machine? There is no longer any answer to this anthropological question' (Baudrillard, 1990).

Conclusion

With the collapse of the rationalist ideology of continuous, linear progress, communication has taken over and flaunts itself as the parameter *par excellence* of the evolution of humanity in an historical period when it is desperately seeking a meaning for its future.

In such a context, contrasting perspectives regarding the question of communication and its actors tend to vanish from the theoretical horizon. Certainly, in the fashionable trend of studying daily life, what is significant, as Georges Balandier notes, is the movement of the mind whereby 'the subject is made to reappear in the face of structures and systems – quality in the face of quantity, lived experience in the face of institutions' (Balandier, 1983), bringing the human and social sciences closer to the 'ordinary subject'.

Yet certain questions concerning the relationship between intellectuals and society have grown blurred in the process. The crisis of utopias and alternatives has struck at the heart of the idea of critical research. Nowadays, every mediator is influenced by managerial positivism, the new utilitarianism spurring the search for epistemological tools to neutralise tensions through technological solutions. Knowledge about communication is no exception to the trend. The rising power of discourses of expertise is carried forward by the increasing professionalism of careers in communication, whose explicit function is to legitimise strategies and models of entrepreneurial and institutional organisation. Of course, there is nothing new about administrative research in the United States. What is novel is its worldwide generalisation, which has accompanied the deregulation of modes of communication. More and more, the pragmatic attitude characterising operational research has permeated communication's modes of expression. As a result, the entire field is finding it increasingly difficult to extricate itself from its instrumental image, and achieve real legitimacy as a full-fledged object of research treated as such with the distance required by a critical approach.

These ideological shifts are undermining the idea that we have entered an age of 'control societies', as Gilles Deleuze called them, borrowing the term from William Burroughs, that is, societies in which the socio-technological mechanisms of flexible control are increasing, inspired by the managerial model of the company as guardian. The control referred to is a control over processes which are in constant, rapid and continual rotation.

The age of the so-called information society is also that of the production of mental states. It will be necessary to rethink the question of freedom and democracy. Political freedom cannot be reduced to the right to exercise one's will. It also lies in the right to control the process whereby that will is formed.

Bibliography

Translators' Note: Where a work is available in English translation, we have quoted from the English text. In such cases page references refer to the translation rather than the original-language edition.

Adorno, T.W. (1969). 'Scientific Experiences of a European Scholar in America', in D. Fleming and B. Baylin (eds), *The Intellectual Migration: Europe and America 1930–1960*, Cambridge, Mass.: Harvard University Press/Belknap.

Adorno, T.W. and Horkheimer, M. (1944). 'The Culture Industry: Enlightenment as Mass Deception', in *Dialectic of Enlightenment*, trans. J. Cumming. New York: Herder & Herder, 1972.

Allemand, E. (1980). *Pouvoir et télévision*. Paris: Anthropos.

Allen, R.C. (1985). *Speaking of Soap Opera*. Chapel Hill: The University of North Carolina Press.

Allen, R.C. (ed.) (1995). *To Be Continued. Soap Operas Around the World*. London: Routledge.

Althabe, G. (1984). *Note Action de recherche*. Paris: CNRS-CENT.

Althusser, L. (1970). 'Idéologie et appareils idéologiques d'état'. *La Pensée* no. 151. (In English, 'Ideology and Ideological State Apparatuses', in *Essays on Ideology*, London: Verso, 1984.)

Althusser, L. et al. (1965). *Lire le Capital*. Paris: Maspero. (In English, *Reading Capital*. London: Verso, 1970).

Ang, I. (1985). *Watching Dallas: Soap Opera and the Melodramatic Imagination*. London: Methuen.

Apparadurai, A. (1990). 'Disjuncture and Difference in the Global Cultural Economy'. *Public Culture* vol. 2, no. 2.

Arnold, M. (1869). *Culture and Anarchy*. Cambridge: Cambridge University Press, 1935.

Austin, J. L. (1962). *How to Do Things with Words*. Oxford: Oxford University Press.

Babbage, C. (1832). *On the Economy of Machinery and Manufactures*. New York: A.M. Kelley, 1963.

Bakhtin, M. [Volosinov, V.N.] (1929). *Marxism and the Philosophy of Language*. New York: The Seminar Press, 1973.

Balandier, G. (1983). 'Essai d'identification du quotidien'. *Cahiers internationaux de sociologie* vol. LXXIV.

Baran, P. (1957). *The Political Economy of Growth*. Harmondsworth: Penguin.

Barthes, R. (1957). *Mythologies*. Paris: Seuil. (In English, *Mythologies*, trans. A. Lavers. London: Cape, 1972.)

Barthes, R. (1964). 'Eléments de sémiologie'. *Communications* no. 4.

Barthes, R. (1967). *Système de la mode*. Paris: Seuil. (In English, *The Fashion System*, trans. M. Ward and R. Howard. New York: Hill & Wang, 1983.)

Barthes, R. (1968). 'La mort de l'auteur', *Mantéia* vol. V. (In English, 'The Death of the Author', in *Image – Music – Text*, trans. S. Heath. London: Fontana, 1977.)

Bateson, G. (1972). *Steps to an Ecology of Mind*. San Francisco: Chandler.

Baudrillard, J. (1972). *Pour une critique de l'économie politique du signe*. Paris: Gallimard. (In English, *For A Critique of the Political Economy of the Sign*, trans. C. Levin. St Louis: Telos Press, 1981.)

Baudrillard, J. (1981). *Simulacres et simulation*. Paris: Galilée.

Baudrillard, J. (1990). *La Transparence du mal*. Paris: Galilée. (In English, *The Transparency of Evil*, trans. J. Benedict. London: Verso, 1993.)

Bauer, R.A., Pool, I. de Sola and Dexter, L.A. (1964). *American Business and Public Policy*. New York: Atherton Press.

Beaud, P. (1984). *La Société de connivence. Médias, médiations et classes sociales*. Paris: Aubier.

Bell, D. (1962). *The End of Ideology*. New York: Free Press.

Bell, D. (1973). *The Coming of Post-Industrial Society: A Venture in Social Forecasting*. New York: Basic Books.

Beltran, L.R. (1976). 'Alien Premises, Objects and Methods in Latin American Communication Research'. *Communication Research* vol. III, no. 2.

Beltrán, L.R. and Fox, E. (1980). *Comunicación dominada. Estados Unidos en los medios de América latina*. Mexico City: Nueva Imagen/ILET.

Beniger, R. (1992). 'Comparison, Yes, But – The Case of Technological and Cultural Change', in J.G. Blumler, J.M. McLeod and K.E. Rosengren, *Comparatively Speaking: Communication across Space and Time*. London: Sage.

Benjamin, W. (1933). 'The Work of Art in the Age of Mechanical Reproduction', in *Illuminations*, H. Arendt (ed.). New York: Schocken Brooks, 1969.

Benjamin, W. (1982). *Das Passagen-Werk*. Frankfurt on Main: Suhrkamp Verlag.

Berelson, B. (1952). *Content Analysis in Communication Research*. New York: Free Press.

Berger, P. and Luckmann, T. (1966). *The Social Construction of Reality: A Treatise in the Sociology of Knowledge*. New York: Doubleday.

Berlo, D.K. (1960). *The Process of Communication: An Introduction to Theory and Practice*. New York: Holt, Rinehart & Winston.

Bertalanffy, L. von (1933). *Modern Theories of Development: Introduction to Theoretical Biology*. Oxford: Oxford University Press.

Bertalanffy, L. von (1968). *General Systems Theory*. New York: Braziller.

Bertillon, A. (1887). *Anthropological Descriptions: New Method of Determining Individual Identity*. Melun (France): Imprimerie administrative.

Bettetini, G. (1983). *La Conversazione audiovisiva*. Milan: Bompiani.

Blumer, H. (1969). *Symbolic Interactionism: Perspective and Method*. Englewood Cliffs, NJ: Prentice-Hall.

Blumler, J. and Katz, E. (eds) (1975). *The Uses and Gratifications Approach to Mass Communication Research*. Annual Review of Communication Research vol. 3. Beverly Hills, Calif.: Sage.

Bordenave, J.D. (1976). 'Communication and Adoption of Agricultural Innovations in Latin America', in R.H. Crawford and W.R. Ward (eds), *Communication Strategies for Rural Development*. Ithaca, NY: Cornell University-CIAT.

Bougnoux, D. (1989). *Vices et vertus des cercles*. Paris: La Découverte.

Boullier, D. (1984). 'Usages du vidéotex et utopie techniciste'. *Réseaux* no. 6, April.

Bourdieu, P. and Passeron, J.C. (1970). *La Reproduction*. Paris: Minuit. (In English, *Reproduction in Education, Society and Culture*, trans. R. Nice. London: Sage, 1990.)

Bourdieu, P. (ed.) (1965). *Un art moyen. Essai sur les usages sociaux de la photographie*. Paris: Minuit.

Bourricaud, F. (1955). 'Introduction'. to T. Parsons, *Élements pour une sociologie de l'action*. Paris: Plon.

Boyd-Barrett, J.O. and Palmer, M. (1980). *Le Trafic des nouvelles. Les agences mondiales d'information*. Paris: A. Moreau.

Braudel, F. (1979). *Civilisation matérielle, économie et capitalisme XVe-XVIIIe*, 3 vols. Paris: A. Colin. (In English, *Civilisation and Capitalism: 15th–18th Centuries*, trans. S. Reynolds. London: Collins, 1981–4).

Breton, P. (1992). *L'Utopie de la communication*. Paris: La Découverte.

Breton, P. and Proulx, S. (1989). *L'Explosion de la communication. La naissance d'une nouvelle idéologie*. Paris: La Découverte.

Brunsdon, C. (1981). 'Crossroads: Notes on a Soap Opera'. *Screen* vol. 22, no. 4.

Brunsdon, C. and Morley, D. (1978). *Everyday Television: Nationwide*. London: BFI.

Brzezinski, Z. (1969). *Between Two Ages: America's Role in the Technetronic Era*. New York: Viking Press.

Bustamante, E. and Zallo, R. (eds) (1988). *Las Industrias culturales en Espana*. Madrid: Akal.

Callon, M. (1986). 'Eléments pour une sociologie de la traduction'. *L'Année sociologique* no. 36.

Cantril, H. Gaudet, H. and Herzog, H. (1940). *The Invasion from Mars*. Princeton, NJ: Princeton University Press.

Capriles, O. (1976). *El Estado y los medios de comunicación en Venezuela*. Caracas: Ininco/Universidad Central de Venezuela.

Carey, J.W. (1983). 'The Origins of the Radical Discourse on Cultural Studies in the United States'. *Journal of Communication* vol. 33, no. 3.

Casetti, F. (1984). *L'Imagine al plurale*. Venice: Marsilio.

Casetti, F. and Odin, R. (1990). 'De la paléo- à la néo-télévision: approche sémio-pragmatique'. *Communications no.* 51.

CECMAS (1966). *Le Centre d'études des communications de masse 1960–1966*. Paris: École des Hautes Etudes (VIe section).

CENECA (1992). *Educación para la comunicación. Manual latinoamericano de educación para los medios de comunicación*. Santiago, Chile: Unesco/Unicef/Ceneca.

Certeau, M. de (1980). *L'Invention du quotidien I. Arts de faire*. Paris: 10/18. (In English, *The Practice of Everyday Life*, trans. S.F. Randall. Berkeley: University of California Press, 1987.)

Cesareo, G. (1974). *La Televisione sprecata*. Milan: Feltrinelli.

Chakhotin, S. (1939). *Le Viol des foules par la propagande politique*. Paris: Gallimard, 1952. (In English, *The Rape of the Masses: The Psychology of Totalitarian Political Propaganda*. New York and London: Routledge, 1940.)

Cicourel, A.V. (1964). *Method and Measurement in Sociology*. New York: Free Press.

Cicourel, A.V. (1980). 'Language and Social Interaction: Philosophical and Empirical Issues'. Working Paper 96, Universita degli Studi di Urbino.

Comte, A. (1830–42). *Cours de philosophie positive*. Paris: Hermann, 1975.

Cooley, C.H. (1909). *Social Organization*. New York: C. Scribner's Sons.

Curran, J. (1990). 'The New Revisionism in Mass Communication Research: A Reappraisal'. *European Journal of Communication* vol. 5, no. 2–3.

Dahlgren, P. (1985). 'Media, Meaning and Method. A "Post-Rational" Perspective'. *Nordicom Review* no. 2.

Dayan, D. (1992). 'Les Mystères de la réception'. *Le Débat* no. 71. Paris.

Debord, G. (1967). *La Société du spectacle*. Paris: Champ libre. (In English, *The Society of the Spectacle*. Detroit: Black & Red, 1977.)

Debray, R. (1979). *Le Pouvoir intellectuel en France*. Paris: Ramsay.

Debray, R. (1991). *Cours de médiologie générale*. Paris: Gallimard.

De Fleur, M.L. (1966). *Theories of Mass Communication*. New York: D. McKay.

Deledalle, G. (1983). *La Philosophie américaine*. Paris: L'Âge d'homme.

Deleuze, G. (1990). *Pourparlers*. Paris: Minuit.

Desrosières, A. (1993). *La Politique des grands nombres. Histoire de la Raison statistique*. Paris: La Découverte.

Deutsch, K. (1953). *Nationalism and Social Communication*. New York: Free Press.

Deutsch, K. (1963). *The Nerves of Government: Models of Political Communication and Control*. New York: Free Press.

Dewey, J. (1927). *The Public and its Problems*. New York: Holt.

Drucker, P. (1993). *Post-Capitalist Society*. Oxford: Butterworth-Heinemann.

Durkheim, E. (1893). *De la Division du travail social*. Paris: Presses Universitaires de France, 1990. (In English, *The Division of Labor in Society*. New York: Free Press, 1933.)

Eagleton, T. (1983). *Literary Theory: An Introduction*. Oxford: Blackwell.

Easton, D. (1965). *Framework for Political Analysis*. Englewood Cliffs, NJ: Prentice-Hall.

Eco, U. (1962). *The Open Work*. London: Hutchinson Radius, 1989.

Eco, U. (1964). *Apocalliti e integrati*. Milan: Bompiani.

Eco, U. (1976). 'Peirce and Contemporary Semantics'. *Versus* no. 15.

Eco, U. (1979). *Lector in fabula: la cooperazione interpretativa nei testi narrativi*. Milan: Bompiani.

Eco, U. (1982). *'Apostille' au Nom de la Rose*. Paris: Grasset.

Elias, N. (1970). *What Is Sociology?* New York: Columbia University Press, 1978.

Ellul, J. (1954). *La Technique ou l'enjeu du siècle*. Paris: A. Colin. (In English, *The Technological Society*. trans. J. Wilkinson, intro. R.K. Merton. New York: Vintage, 1964.)

Ellul, J. (1977). *Le Système technicien*. Paris: Calmann-Lévy.

Enzensberger, H.M. (1970). 'Constituents of a Theory of the Media'. *New Left Review* December.

Escarpit, R. (ed.) (1970). *Le Littéraire et le social. Eléments pour une sociologie de la Littérature*. Paris: Flammarion.

Ewald, F. (1986). *L'État Providence*. Paris: Grasset.

Ewen, S. (1976). *The Captains of Consciousness*. New York: McGraw-Hill.

Fabbri, P. (1973). 'Le comunicazioni di massa in Italia: sguardo semiotico e malocchio della sociologia'. *VS* no. 5.

Fiske, J. (1987). *Television Culture*. London: Methuen.

Flichy, P. (1980). *Les Industries de l'imaginaire*. Grenoble: Presses Universitaires de Grenoble.

Flichy, P. (1991). *Une Histoire de la communication moderne*. Paris: La Découverte. (In English, *Dynamics of Modern Communication: The Shaping and Impact of New Communication Technology*, trans. Liz Libbrecht. London: Sage, 1995.)

Fornel, M. de (ed.) (1988). 'L'interaction communicationnelle'. *Réseaux* no. 29, March.

Foucault, M. (1966). *Les Mots et les choses*. Paris, Gallimard. (In English, *The Order of Things: An Archaeology of the Human Sciences*, trans. A. Sheridan. London: Tavistock Publications, 1970; Routledge, 1993.)

Foucault, M. (1975). *Surveiller et punir*. Paris: Gallimard. (In English, *Discipline and Punish: The Birth of the Prison*, trans. A. Sheridan. London: Penguin, 1977.)

Foucault, M. (1986). 'La gouvernementalité'. *Actes. Les Cahiers d'action juridique* no. 54.

Freire, P. (1970). *Pedagogy of the Oppressed*, trans. M.B. Ramos. New York: Seabury Press, 1974.

Freud, S. (1921). 'Group Psychology and the Analysis of the Ego', in *The Complete Psychological Works of Sigmund Freud*, vol. 18, trans. J. Strachey in collaboration with A. Freud. London: Hogarth Press and the Institute of Psychoanalysis, 1955.

Friedmann, G. (1966a). *Sept études sur l'homme et la technique*. Paris: Gonthier.

Friedmann, G. (1966b). 'La Sociologie des communications de masse', in *Aspects de la sociologie française*. Paris: Éditions Ouvrières.

Fuenzalida, V. and Hermosilla, M.E. (1991). *El televidente activo. Manual para la recepción activa de TV. Santiago*. Chile: Corporación de Promoción Universitaria, Fundación Adenauer.

Fukuyama, F. (1992). *The End of History and the Last Man*. New York: Free Press.

Galton, F. (1889). *Essays in Eugenics*. London: Macmillan.

Galtung, J. (1971). 'A Structural Theory of Imperialism'. *Journal of Peace Research* no. 2.

García Canclini, N. (1990). *Culturas híbridas. Estrategias para entrar y salir de la modernidad*. Mexico: Grijalbo. (In English, *Hybrid Cultures: Strategies for Entering and Leaving Modernity*, trans. C.L. Chiappari and S.L. Lopez. Minneapolis: University of Minnesota Press, 1995.)

Garfinkel, H. (1967). *Studies in Ethnomethodology*. Englewood Cliffs, NJ: Prentice-Hall.

Garnham, N. (1979). 'Contribution to a Political Economy of Mass Communication'. *Media, Culture & Society* vol. I, no. 2, April.

Garnham, N. (1983). 'Toward a Theory of Cultural Materialism'. *Journal of Communication* vol. 33, no. 3, Summer.

Garnham, N. (1990). *Capitalism and Global Communication: Global Culture and the Politics of Information*. London: Sage.

Garnham, N. (1995). 'Political Economy and Cultural Studies: Reconciliation or Divorce'. *Critical Studies in Mass Communication* vol. 12, no. 1.

Gay, P. du (ed.) (1997). *Production of Culture/Cultures of Production*. London: Sage.

Geertz, C. (1973). *The Interpretation of Cultures*. New York: Basic Books.

Gerbner, G. (ed.) (1983) 'Ferment in the Field: Communications Scholars Address Critical Issues and Research Tasks of the Discipline'. *Journal of Communication* vol. 33, no. 3, Summer.

Giddens, A. (1984). *The Constitution of Society: Outline of the Theory of Structuration*. Cambridge: Polity Press.

Giraud, A., Wolton, D. and Missika, J.L. (eds) (1978). *Les Réseaux pensants*. Paris: Masson.

Girsic (Groupe Inter-Universitaire de Recherche en Science de l'Information et de la Communication) (ed.) (1994). *Pour une nouvelle économie du savoir*. Rennes: Presses Universitaires de Rennes.

Gitlin, T. (1979). 'Media Sociology: The Dominant Paradigm'. *Theory and Society* vol. 6, no. 2.

Goffman, E. (1967). *Interaction Ritual: Essays on Face-to-Face Behaviour*. New York: Doubleday.

Goffman, E. (1971). *Relations in Public: Microstudies of the Public Order*. New York: Basic Books.

Golding, P. (1974). 'Media Role in National Development: Critique of a Theoretical Orthodoxy'. *Journal of Communication* vol. 24, no. 3.

Golding, P. and Murdock, G. (1991). 'Culture, Communication, and Political

Economy', in J. Curran and M. Gurevitch (eds), in *Mass Media and Society*. London: Edward Arnold.

Goldmann, L. (1959). *Le Dieu caché*. Paris: Gallimard. (In English, *The Hidden God*. London: Routledge & Kegan Paul, 1964.)

Goody, J. (1977). *The Domestication of the Savage Mind*. Cambridge: Cambridge University Press.

Gramsci, A. (1971). *Selections from the Prison Notebooks*, Q. Hoare and G. Nowell Smith (eds). London: Lawrence and Wishart.

Grandi, R. and Richeri, G. (1976). *Le Televisioni in Europa*. Milan: Feltrinelli.

Gregory, D. (1993). *Geographical Imaginations*. Oxford: Blackwell.

Greimas, A.J. (1966). *Sémantique structurale*. Paris: Larousse.

Grewal, I. and Kaplan, C. (eds). (1994). *Scattered Hegemonies: Postmodernity and Transnational Feminist Practices*. Minneapolis: University of Minnesota Press.

Grossberg, L. (1995). 'Cultural Studies vs. Political Economy: Is Anybody Else Bored with this Debate?'. *Critical Studies in Mass Communication* vol. 12, no. 1.

Guattari, F. (1987). 'Les Nouveaux mondes du capitalisme'. *Libération*, 22 December.

Guattari, F. (1992). *Chaosmose*. Paris: Galilée.

Guback, T. (1969). *The International Film Industry: Western Europe and America since 1945*. Bloomington: Indiana University Press.

Gubern, R. (1972). *El Lenguaje de los comics*. Barcelona: Peninsula.

Habermas, J. (1962). *Strukturwandel der Öffentlichkeit*. Darmstadt: Hermann Luchterhand Verlag. (In English, *The Structural Transformation of the Public Sphere: An Inquiry into a Category of Bourgeois Society*, trans. T. Burger and F. Lawrence. Cambridge, Mass.: MIT Press, 1989.)

Habermas, J. (1968). *Technik und Wissenschaft als Ideologie*. Frankfurt: Suhrkamp Verlag.

Habermas, J. (1981). *Theorie des Kommunikativen Handelns*. Frankfurt: Suhrkamp Verlag. (In English, *The Theory of Communicative Action*, 2 vols. Boston: Beacon Press, 1984, 1987.)

Hall, E.T. (1959). *The Silent Language*. New York: Doubleday.

Hall, E.T. (1971). *The Hidden Dimension*. New York: Doubleday.

Hall, S. (1980). 'Encoding/Decoding'. In S. Hall, D. Hobson, A. Lowe and P. Willis (eds), *Culture, Media, Language*. London: Hutchinson University Library.

Hall, S. and Whannel, P. (1964). *The Popular Arts*. London: Hutchinson.

Hamelink, C. (ed.) (1977). *The Corporate Village: The Role of Transnational Corporations in International Communication*. Rome: IDOC.

Heritage, J. (1987). 'Ethnomethodology', in A. Giddens and J. Turner (eds), *Social Theory Today*. Cambridge: Polity Press.

Hoggart, R. (1957). *The Uses of Literacy*. Fairlawn, NJ: Essential Books.

Horkheimer, M. (1972). *Critical Theory: Selected Essays*. New York: Seabury Press.

Hovland, C., Janis I. and Kelley, H. (1953). *Communication and Persuasion*. New Haven, Conn.: Yale University Press.

Innis, H.A. (1950). *Empire and Communications*. Toronto: University of Toronto Press.

Innis, H.A. (1951). *The Bias of Communication*. Toronto: University of Toronto Press.

Iribarne, P. d' (1989). *La Logique de l'honneur: gestion des entreprises et traditions nationales*. Paris: Seuil.

Iser, W. (1972). *The Implied Reader.* Baltimore, Md: Johns Hopkins University Press, 1974.

Iser, W. (1976). *The Act of Reading*. Baltimore and London: Johns Hopkins University Press, 1978.

Jacob, F. (1970). *La Logique du vivant*. Paris: Gallimard. (In English, *The Logic of Life: A History of Heredity*, trans. B.E. Spillmann. New York: Vintage, 1973.)

Jakobson, R. (1962). *Selected Writings*, 4 vols. The Hague: Mouton.

Jameson, F. (1984). 'Postmodernism, or the Cultural Logic of Late Capitalism', *New Left Review*, July–August.

Jauss, H.R. (1970). *Toward an Aesthetic of Reception*, trans. T. Bahti. Minneapolis: University of Minnesota Press, 1982.

Javeau, C. (1986). 'George Simmel et la vie quotidienne: *Tür* et *Brücke* et socialité', in P. Watier (ed.), *Georg Simmel et l'expérience du monde moderne*. Paris: Méridiens-Klincksieck.

Jouët, J. (1987). *L'Ecran apprivoisé. Télématique et informatique à domicile*. Paris: CNET-Réseaux.

Jouët, J. (1993). 'Pratiques de communication et figures de la médiation'. *Réseaux* no. 60, July–August.

Kaplan, A. (ed.) (1983). *Regarding Television: Critical Approaches*. Frederick, Md: University Publications of America.

Katz, E. (1957). 'The Two-Step Flow of Communication: An Up-to-Date Report on an Hypothesis'. *Public Opinion Quarterly* vol. 21.

Katz, E. (1990). 'À propos des médias et de leurs effets', in L. Sfez and G. Coutlée (eds), *Technologies et symboliques de la communication*. Grenoble: Presses Universitaires de Grenoble.

Katz, E. and Lazarsfeld, P.F. (1955). *Personal Influence: The Part Played by People in the Flow of Mass Communication*. Glencoe, Ill.: Free Press, 1970.

Keane, J. (1990). *The Media and Democracy.* Cambridge: Polity Press.

Kracauer, S. (1922–25). *Der Detektiv-Roman*, in *Schriften*. Frankfurt on Main: Suhrkamp Verlag, 1971.

Lacroix, J.G. and Lévesque, B. (eds) (1986). 'Les Industries culturelles: un enjeu vital'. *Cahiers de recherche sociologique* vol. 4, no. 2. Montréal.

Lasswell, H. (1927). *Propaganda Technique in the World War.* New York: Knopf.

Lasswell, H. (1935). *World Politics and Personal Insecurity.* New York: McGraw-Hill.

Lasswell, H. (1948). 'The Structure and Function of Communication in Society', in L. Bryson (ed.), *The Communication of Ideas*. New York: Harper.

Lasswell, H. (1963). *The Future of Political Science*. New York: Atherton Press.

Latour, B. (1987). *Science in Action*. Milton Keynes: Open University Press/Cambridge, Mass.: Harvard University Press.

Laulan, A.M. (1986). 'La Résistance aux systèmes d'information'. *Réseaux* no. 19, May.

Lazarsfeld, P.F. (1941). 'Remarks on Administrative and Critical Communications Research'. *Studies in Philosophy and Social Sciences* vol. 9, no. 1.

Lazarsfeld, P.F. (1953). 'The Prognosis for International Communication Research'. *Public Opinion Quarterly* vol. 16.

Lazarsfeld, P.F. and Rosenberg, M. (1955). *The Language of Social Research*. New York: Colliers.

Lazarsfeld, P.F., Berelson, B. and Gaudet, H. (1944). *The People's Choice*. New York: Duell, Sloan & Pearce.

Lazarsfeld, P.F., Jahoda, M. and Zeisel, H. (1932). *Les Chômeurs de Marienthal*. Paris: Minuit, 1981.

Leavis, F.R. (1930). *Mass Civilisation and Minority Culture*. London: Chatto and Windus.

Leavis, F.R. (1943). 'Education and the University', in *Collected Essays*. London: Chatto and Windus.

Le Bon, G. (1894). *Lois psychologiques de l'évolution des peuples*. Paris: Alcan.

Le Bon, G. (1895). *Psychologie des foules*. Paris: Presses Universitaires de France, 1988. (In English, *The Crowd: A Study in the Popular Mind*. Dunwoody, Ga: Norman S. Berg, 1977, 2nd edn.)

Lefebvre, H. (1947, 1962, 1981). *Critique de la vie quotidienne*, 3 vols. Paris: L'Arche. (In English, *Critique of Everyday Life*. London: Verso, vol. 1, 1991.)

Lefebvre, H. (1967). *Position: Contre les technocrates*. Paris: Gonthier.

Lerner, D. (1958). *The Passing of Traditional Society: Modernizing the Middle East*. Glencoe, Ill.: Free Press.

Lévi-Strauss, C. (1949). *Les Structures élémentaires de la parenté*. Paris: Presses universitaires de France.

Lévi-Strauss, C. (1958 and 1973). *Anthropologie structurale*, 2 vols. Paris: Plon. (In English, *Structural Anthropology*, 2 vols. Harmondsworth: Penguin, 1994.)

Levitt, T. (1983). 'The Globalization of Markets'. *Harvard Business Review*, May–June.

Lévy, P. (1990). *Les Technologies de l'intelligence*. Paris: La Découverte.

Lévy, P. (1994). *L'Intelligence collective*. Paris: La Découverte.

Lewin, K. (1935). *A Dynamic Theory of Personality*. New York: McGraw-Hill.

Lewin, K. (1936). *Principles of Topological Psychology*. New York: McGraw-Hill.

Liebes, T. and Katz, E. (1991). *The Export of Meaning: Cross-Cultural Readings of Dallas*. Oxford: Oxford University Press.

Lombroso, C. (1876). *L'Homme criminel. Étude anthropologique et médicale*. Paris: Alcan, 1887.

Löwenthal, L. (1944). 'Biographies in Popular Magazines', in P.F. Lazarsfeld and F. Stanton (eds), *Radio Research 1942–43*. New York: Duell, Sloan.

Luhmann, N. (1991). 'Communication et action'. *Réseaux* no. 50, November–December.

Lukács, G. (1923). *History and Class Consciousness: Studies in Marxist Dialectics*, trans. R. Livingstone. Cambridge, Mass.: MIT Press, 1971.

Lull, J. (ed.) (1988). *World Families Watch Television*. London: Sage.

Lyotard, F. (1979). *La Condition postmoderne*. Paris: Minuit. (In English, *The Postmodern Condition: A Report on Knowledge*, trans. G. Bennington and B. Massumi. Minneapolis: University of Minnesota Press, 1984.)

MacBride, S. (Commission) (1980). *Many Voices, One World*. Paris: Unesco.

MacDonald, D. (1944). 'A Theory of Mass Culture'. *Politics*, February.

MacDonald, D. (1963). *Against the American Grain*. New York: Vintage Books.

McDougall, W. (1920). *The Group Mind*. Cambridge: Cambridge University Press.

McGuigan, J. (1992). *Cultural Populism*. London: Routledge.

Machlup, F. (1962). *The Production and Distribution of Knowledge in the United States*. Princeton, NJ: Princeton University Press.

McLuhan, M. (1962). *The Gutenberg Galaxy*. Toronto: University of Toronto Press.

McLuhan, M. (1964). *Understanding Media*. New York: McGraw-Hill.

McLuhan, M. and Fiore, Q. (1969). *War and Peace in the Global Village*. New York: Bantam.

Marcuse, H. (1964). *One-Dimensional Man*. Boston: Beacon Press.

Marsal, J. (1977). *La Crisis de la sociología norteamericana*. Barcelona: Península.

Martín Barbero, J. (1987). *De los medios a las mediaciones*. Barcelona: G. Gili. (In English, *Communication, Culture and Hegemony: From the Media to the Mediations*, trans. E. Fox. London: Sage, 1993.)

Martín Barbero, J. and Muñoz, S. (eds) (1992). *Televisión y melodrama*. Bogotá: Tercer Mundo Editores.

Mattelart, A. (1974). *Mass media, idéologies et le mouvement révolutionnaire*. Paris: Anthropos. (In English, *Mass Media, Ideologies and the Revolutionary Movement. Chile 1970–1973*, trans. M. Coad. Brighton: Harvester Press, 1980.)

Mattelart, A. (1976). *Multinationales et systèmes de communication*. Paris: Anthropos. (In English, *Multinational Corporations and the Control of Culture*, trans. M. Chanan. Brighton: Harvester Press, 1979.)

Mattelart, A. (1992). *La Communication-monde. Histoire des idées et des stratégies*. Paris: La Découverte. (In English, *Mapping World Communication: War, Progress, Culture*, trans. S. Emanuel and J.A. Cohen. Minneapolis: University of Minnesota Press.)

Mattelart, A. (1994). *L'Invention de la communication*. Paris: La Découverte. (In English, *The Invention of Communication*, trans. S. Emanuel. Minneapolis: University of Minnesota Press, 1996.)

Mattelart, A. and Mattelart, M. (1979). *De l'usage des médias en temps de crise*. Paris: A. Moreau.

Mattelart, A. and Mattelart, M. (1986). *Penser les médias*. Paris: La Découverte. (In English, *Rethinking Media Theory*, trans. M. Urquidi and J.A. Cohen. Minneapolis: University of Minnesota Press, 1992.)

Mattelart, A. and Neveu, E. (1996). '"Cultural Studies" stories: vers la domestication d'une pensée sauvage?' *Réseaux* no. 80, November–December.

Mattelart, A. and Piemme, J.M. (1980). 'New Means of Communication: New Questions for the Left'. *Media, Culture & Society* no. 2.

Mattelart, A., Mattelart, M. and Delcourt, X. (1983). *La Culture contre la démocratie? L'audiovisuel à l'ère transnationale.* Paris: La Découverte. (In English, *International Image Markets: In Search of an Alternative Perspective*, trans. D. Buxton. London: Comedia, 1984.)

Mattelart, M. (1986). *Women, Media, Crisis: Femininity and Disorder.* London: Comedia/Methuen.

Mattelart, M. and Mattelart, A. (1987). *Le Carnaval des images.* Paris: INA-La Documentation française. (In English, *The Carnival of Images: Brazilian Television Fiction*, trans. D. Buxton. New York: Bergin and Garvey/Greenwood, 1990.)

Maturana, H. and Varela, F. (1980). *Autopoiesis and Cognition.* Boston: D. Reidel.

Mayo, E. (1933). *The Human Problems of an Industrial Civilization.* New York: Macmillan.

Mazziotti, N. (1996). *La Industria de la telenovela.* Buenos Aires: Paidos.

Mead, G.H. (1934). *Mind, Self and Society.* Chicago: University of Chicago Press.

Merleau-Ponty, M. (1945). *Phénoménologie de la perception.* Paris: Gallimard, 1989. (In English, *The Phenomenology of Perception.* London: Routledge and Kegan Paul, 1962.)

Merton, R.K. (1949). *Social Theory and Social Structure.* Glencoe, Ill.: Free Press.

Metz, C. (1968, 1972). *Essais sur la signification au cinéma*, 2 vols. Paris: Klincksieck.

Miège, B. (1989a). *La Société conquise par la communication.* Grenoble: Presses Universitaires de Grenoble.

Miège, B. (1989b). *The Capitalization of Cultural Production.* New York: International General Editions.

Miège, B. (ed.) (1990). *Médias et communication en Europe.* Grenoble: Presses Universitaires de Grenoble.

Miège, B., Huet, A., Ion J., Lefebvre, A. and Peron, R. (1978). *Capitalisme et industries culturelles.* Grenoble: Presses Universitaires de Grenoble.

Mill, J.S. (1848). *Principles of Political Economy with Some of Their Applications to Social Philosophy*, W.J. Ashley (ed.). Toronto and New York: University of Toronto Press/Routledge and Kegan Paul.

Mills, C.W. (1956). *The Power Elite.* New York: Oxford University Press.

Mills, C.W. (1959). *The Sociological Imagination.* Harmondsworth: Penguin, 1970.

Mills, C.W. (1963). *Power, Politics and People.* New York: Oxford University Press.

Modleski, T. (1984). *Loving With a Vengeance: Mass-Produced Fantasies for Women.* London: Methuen.

Moeglin, P. (1991). 'Télématique: de la recherche sur les usages aux usages de la recherche'. *Bulletin du CERTEIC* no. 12, May.

Moeglin, P. (1994). *Le Satellite éducatif. Média et expérimentation.* Paris: Coll. Réseaux/CNET.

Moles, A. (1975). 'Le mur de la communication'. *Actes du XVe Congrès de la ASPLF* vol. II.

Moragas, M. de (1976). *Semiótica y communicación de masas*. Barcelona: Peninsula/Edicions 62.

Moreno, J.P. (1934). *Who Shall Survive? Foundations of Sociometry Group Psychotherapy and Sociodrama*. Washington: Nervous and Mental Disease Monograph no. 58.

Morin, E. (1956). *Le Cinéma ou l'homme imaginaire*. Paris: Minuit.

Morin, E. (1957). *Les Stars*. Paris: Seuil.

Morin, E. (1962). *L'Esprit du temps*. Paris: Grasset.

Morin, E. (1991). *La Méthode*. Vol. 4: *Les Idées*. Paris: Seuil.

Morley, D. (1980). *The Nationwide Audience: Structure and Decoding*. London: BFI.

Morley, D. (1986). *Family Television: Cultural Power and Domestic Leisure*. London: Routledge (Comedia).

Morley, D. (1992). *Television, Audiences and Cultural Studies*. London: Routledge.

Morley, D. and Robins, K. (1995). *Spaces of Identity: Global Media, Electronic Landscapes and Cultural Boundaries*. London: Routledge.

Mosco, V. (1996). *The Political Economy of Communication*. London: Sage.

Mowlana, H. and Wilson, L.J. (1990). *The Passing of Modernity: Communication and the Transformation of Society*. New York and London: Longman.

Mulvey, L. (1975). 'Visual Pleasure and Narrative Cinema'. *Screen* vol. 16, no. 3.

Musso, P. (1990). 'Métaphores du réseau et de l'organisme: la transition saint-simonienne' in L. Sfez, G. Coutlée and P. Musso (eds), *Technologies et symboliques de la communication*. Grenoble: Presses Universitaires de Grenoble.

Neveu, E. (1994). *Une société de communication?* Paris: Montchrestien.

Nora, S. and Minc, A. (1979). *L'Informatisation de la société*. Paris: La Documentation française.

Nordenstreng, K. and Schiller, H. (eds) (1993). *Beyond National Sovereignty: International Communications in the 1990s*. Norwood, NJ: Ablex.

Nordenstreng, K. and Varis, T. (1974). *Television Traffic – A One-Way Street?* Paris: Unesco.

Ohmae, K. (1985). *Triad Power*. New York: Free Press.

Orozco Gómez, G. (1996a). *Televisión y audiencias. Un enfoque cualitativo*. Madrid/Mexico City: Ediciones de la Torre/Universidad Iberoamericana.

Orozco Gómez, G. (1996b). *Miradas latinoamericanas a la televisión*. Mexico City: Universidad Iberoamericana.

Ortiz, R. (1988). *A Moderna Tradição Brasileira*. São Paulo: Brasiliense.

Oritz, R., Borelli, S.H. and Ortiz Ramos, J. (1989). *Telenovela, historia e produção*. São Paulo: Brasiliense.

Osgood, C., Suci, G. and Tannenbaum, P. (1957). *The Measurement of Meaning*. Urbana, Ill.: University of Illinois Press,

Park, R.E. (1922). *The Immigrant Press and its Control*. New York: Harper.

Park, R.E. (1936). 'Human Ecology'. *The American Journal of Sociology*, vol. XXLII. July.

Park, R.E. and Burgess, E. (1921). *Introduction to the Science of Sociology.* Chicago: University of Chicago Press.

Parsons, T. (1937). *The Structure of Social Action.* New York: McGraw-Hill.

Pasquali, A. (1963). *Comunicación y cultura de masas.* Caracas: Monte Avila.

Pavlov, I. (1929). *Leçons sur l'activité du cortex cérébral.* Paris: Legrand. (In English, see K. Kochoiantz (ed.), *Selected Works.* Moscow: Foreign Language Editions, 1954.)

Peirce, C.W. (1932). *Collected Papers of C.S. Peirce* vol. 2, C. Harsthorne and P. Weiss (eds). Cambridge, Mass.: Harvard University Press.

Perriault, J. (1989). *La Logique de l'usage: essai sur les machines à communiquer.* Paris: Flammarion.

Piemme, J.M. (1980). *La Télévision comme on la parle.* Brussels/Paris: Labor/Nathan.

Pollak, M. (1979). 'Paul Lazarsfeld, fondateur d'une multinationale scientifique'. *Actes de la recherche en sciences sociales* no. 25.

Pool, I. de Sola (1963). 'Le rôle de la communication dans le processus de la modernisation et du changement technologique', in B. Hoselitz and W. Moore (eds), *Industrialisation et société.* Paris: Unesco.

Pool, I. de Sola (ed.) (1974). *Talking Back: Citizen Feed-Back and Cable Technology.* Cambridge, Mass.: MIT Press.

Porat, M.U. (1977). *The Information Economy: Definition and Measurement.* 9 vols. Washington, DC: Government Printing Office.

Preston, W., Herman, E.S. and Schiller, H. (1989). *Hope and Folly: The United States and Unesco, 1945–1985.* Minneapolis: University of Minnesota Press.

Quéré, L. (1982). *Les Miroirs équivoques. Aux origines de la communication moderne.* Paris: Aubier.

Quéré, L. (1988). 'Sociabilité et interaction sociales', *Réseaux* no. 29.

Quéré, L. (1989). 'Les Boîtes noires de B. Latour ou le lien social dans la machine', *Réseaux* no. 36, June.

Quesnay, F. (1758). 'Le Tableau économique', in *Oeuvres économiques et philosophiques de F. Quesnay,* A. Oncken (ed.). Paris: Jules Peelman, 1888.

Quételet, A. (1835). *Sur l'homme et le développement de ses facultés ou essai de physique sociale.* 2 vols. Paris: Bachelier.

Raboy, M. and Dagenais, B. (eds) (1992). *Media, Crisis and Democracy: Mass Communication and the Disruption of Social Order.* London: Sage.

Radcliffe-Brown, A.R. (1961). *Structure and Function in Primitive Society.* London: Cohen & West.

Radway, J. (1984). *Reading the Romance: Women, Patriarchy and Popular Literature.* Chapel Hill: University of North Carolina Press.

Ratzel, F. (1897). *Politische Geographie.* Munich: Oldenburg.

Reich, W. (1933). *The Mass Psychology of Fascism.* New York: Farrar, Strauss & Giroux, 1971.

Roach, C. (1997). 'Cultural Imperialism and Resistance'. *Media, Culture and Society* no. 2.

Rogers, E. (1962). *The Diffusion of Innovations*. Glencoe, Ill.: Free Press.

Rogers, E. (1976). 'Communication and Development: The Passing of the Dominant Paradigm'. *Communication Research* vol. 2, no. 2.

Rogers, E. (1982). 'The Empirical and the Critical Schools of Communication Research', in M. Burgoon (ed.), *Communication Yearbook* no. 5. New Brunswick, NJ: Transaction Books.

Rogers, E. and Kincaid, L. (1981). *Communication Networks: Toward a New Paradigm for Research*. New York: Free Press.

Sacks, H. (1963). 'Sociological Description'. *Berkeley Journal of Sociology* no. 8.

Saint-Simon, H. de (1966). *Oeuvres de Saint-Simon et Enfantin*, 6 vols, reprint. Paris: Anthropos.

Sarló, B. (1985). *El Imperio de los sentimientos*. Buenos Aires: Catalogos Ediciones.

Sartre, J.-P. (1947). *Qu'est-ce que la littérature?* Paris: Gallimard, 1985.

Sartre, J.-P. (1960). 'Questions de méthode', in *Critique de la raison dialectique* vol. 1. Paris: Gallimard.

Sartre, J.-P. (1963). *The Problem of Method*. London: Methuen.

Sartre, J.-P. (1990). *What is Literature?* London: Routledge.

Saussure, F. de (1915). *Cours de linguistique générale (1906–1911)*. Paris: Payot, 1962. (In English, *A Course in General Linguistics*. London: Fontana, 1974.)

Schiller, H. (1969). *Mass Communications and American Empire*. Boston: Beacon Press.

Schiller, H. (1976). *Communication and Cultural Domination*. New York: Sharpe.

Schiller, H. (1989). *Culture Inc.: The Corporate Takeover of Public Expression*. New York and Oxford: Oxford University Press.

Schiller, D. (1996). *Theorizing Communication*. Oxford: Oxford University Press.

Schlesinger, P. (1991). *Media, State, Nation: Political Violence and Collective Identities*. London: Sage.

Schmucler, H. (1974). 'La investigación sobre comunicación masiva'. *Comunicación y Cultura* no. 4. Buenos Aires.

Schmucler, H. (1997). *Memoria de la comunicación*. Buenos Aires: Editorial Biblos.

Schramm, W. (1964). *Mass Media and National Development: The Role of Information in Developing Countries*. Stanford: Stanford University Press.

Schramm, W. (ed.) (1970). *The Process and Effects of Mass Communication*. Urbana: University of Illinois Press.

Schrödinger, E. (1943). *What Is Life?* New York: Doubleday, 1956.

Schütz, A. (1971). *Collected Papers*. The Hague: Martinus Nijhoff.

Serrano, M.M. (1977). *La Mediación social*. Madrid: Akal.

Sfez, L. (1988). *Critique de la communication*. Paris: Seuil.

Shannon, C. and Weaver, W. (1949). *The Mathematical Theory of Communication*. Urbana and Champaign, Ill.: University of Illinois Press.

Shils, E. (1960). 'Mass Society and its Culture'. *Daedalus* vol. 89, no. 2.

Shils, E. (1972). *The Intellectuals and the Powers and Other Essays*. Chicago: University of Chicago Press.

Sighele, S. (1891). *La Foule criminelle. Essai de psychologie collective.* Paris: Alcan, 1901 (2nd edn).

Silverstone, R. (1994). *Television and Everyday Life.* London: Routledge.

Simmel, G. (1903). 'Métropoles et mentalité' in Y. Grafmeyer and I. Joseph (eds), *L'École de Chicago.* Paris: Éditions du Champ urbain, 1971, and Aubier, 1984.

Simmel, G. (1908). 'Digressions sur l'étranger' in Y. Grafmeyer and I. Joseph (eds), *L'École de Chicago.* Paris: Éditions du Champ urbain, 1971, and Aubier, 1984.

Simmel, G. (1964). *The Web of Group-Affiliations,* trans. R. Bendix. New York: Free Press.

Simondon, G. (1969). *Du Mode d'existence des objets techniques.* Paris: Aubier.

Slack, J.D. and Allor, M. (1983). 'The Political and Epistemological Constituents of Critical Communication Research'. *Journal of Communication* vol. 33, no. 3.

Smith, A. (1776). *An Inquiry into the Nature and Causes of the Wealth of Nations.* London: Methuen, 1930.

Smythe, D.W. (1977). 'Communication: A Blindspot of Western Marxism'. *Canadian Journal of Political and Social Theory* vol. I, no. 3.

Smythe, D. (1981). *Dependency Road: Communication, Capitalism, Consciousness and Canada.* Norwood, NJ: Ablex.

Spencer, H. (1876–96). *Principles of Sociology.* 3 vols. London: Williams & Norgate.

Stiegler, B. (1994). *La Technique et le temps* vol. 1. Paris: Galilée.

Stourdzé, Y. (1987; original 1978). 'Généalogie des télécommunications françaises', in *Pour une poignée d'électrons. Pouvoir et communication.* Paris: Fayard. (Also in A. Giraud, D. Wolton and J.L. Missika (eds), *Les Réseaux pensants.* Paris: Masson, 1978.)

Tarde, G. (1890). *Les Lois de l'imitation. Étude sociologique.* Paris: Alcan, 1901. (In English, *The Laws of Imitation,* trans. E.C. Parsons. New York: Henry Holt.)

Tarde, G. (1901). *L'Opinion et la foule.* Paris: Alcan.

Tehranian, M. (1994). 'Where is the New World Order: at the End of History or Clash of Civilisations?', *The Journal of International Communication* vol. 1, no. 2.

Thompson, E.P. (1968). *The Making of the English Working Class.* Harmondsworth: Penguin.

Thompson, J.B. (1995). *The Media and Modernity: A Social Theory of the Media.* Cambridge: Polity Press.

Tiercelin, C. (1993). *C.S. Peirce et le pragmatisme.* Paris: Presses Universitaires de France.

Tomlinson, J. (1991). *Cultural Imperialism. A Critical Introduction.* London: Pinter.

Tremblay, G. (ed.) (1990). *Les Industries de la culture et de la communication au Québec et au Canada.* Montréal: Presses de l'Université du Québec.

Tunstall, J. (1977). *The Media Are American.* London: Constable.

Varela, F. (1989). *Connaître les sciences cognitives.* Paris: Seuil.

Varela, V., Thompson, E. and Rosch, E. (1993). *L'Inscription corporelle de l'esprit. Sciences cognitives et expérience humaine.* Paris: Seuil.

Vattimo, G. (1989). *La Società trasparente.* Turin: Garzanti Editore. (In English, *The Transparent Society.* Cambridge: Polity Press, 1992.)

Vedel, T. (1994). 'Sociologie des innovations technologiques et usagers: introduction à une socio-politique des usages', in A. Vitalis (ed.), *Médias et nouvelles technologies. Pour une socio-politique des usages*. Rennes: Apogée (CERCI-Rennes 2).

Veron, E. (1988). *La Semiosis sociale*. Paris: Presses Universitaires de Vincennes.

Vincent, J.-M. (1990). 'La sociologie en contrepoint'. *L'Homme et la société* no. 97.

Virilio, P. (1990). *L'Inertie polaire*. Paris: Christian Bourgois.

Vitalis, A. (ed.) (1994). *Médias et nouvelles technologies. Pour une socio-politique des usages*. Rennes: Apogée (CERCI-Rennes 2).

Wallerstein, I. (1983). *Historical Capitalism*. London: Verso.

Wartella, E. and Reeves, B. (1985). 'Historical Trends in Research on Children and the Media: 1990–1960'. *Journal of Communication* vol. 35, no. 2, Spring.

Wasko, J., Mosco, V. and Pendakur, M. (1993). *Illuminating the Blindspots. Essays Honoring Dallas W. Smythe*. Norwood, NJ: Ablex.

Watson, J. (1914). *Behavior: An Introduction to Comparative Psychology*. New York: Holt.

Watzlawick, P., Beavin, J.H. and Jackson, D.D. (1967). *Pragmatics of Human Communication*. New York: Norton.

Webster, F. and Robins, K. (1989). 'Towards a Cultural History of the Information Society'. *Theory and Society* no. 18.

Westley, B. and McLean, M. (1957). 'A Conceptual Model of Communication Research'. *Journalism Quarterly* no. 34.

Wiener, N. (1948). *Cybernetics or Control and Communication in the Animal and the Machine*. Paris: Hermann.

Williams, R.(1958). *Culture and Society: 1780–1950*. Harmondsworth, Penguin, 1961.

Williams, R. (1960). 'Advertising: The Magic System'. *New Left Review* no. 4.

Williams, R. (1965). *The Long Revolution*. Harmondsworth: Penguin.

Williams, R. (1974). *Television: Technology and Cultural Form*. London: Fontana.

Williams, R. (1981). *The Sociology of Culture*. New York: Schocken Books.

Winkin, Y. (ed.) (1984). *La Nouvelle communication*. Paris: Seuil.

Wittgenstein, L. (1953). *Philosophical Investigations*. Oxford: Blackwell, 1963.

Wolf, M. (1977). *Gli Apparati delle communicazioni di massa*. Bologna: Guaraldi.

Wolf, M. (1990). *Le Discrete influenze. Gli effeti a lungo termine dei media*. Milan: Bompiani.

Selected anthologies and textbooks

Brunsdon, C., D'Acci J., and Spigel, L. (eds) (1997). *Feminist Television Criticism. A Reader*. Oxford: Oxford University Press.

Bougnoux, D. (ed.) (1993). *Sciences de l'information de la communication. Textes essentiels*. Paris: Larousse.

Boure, R. and Pailliart, I. (eds) (1992), *Les Théories de la communication*. Paris: CinémAction no. 63, March.

Collins, R., Curran, J., Garnham, N., Scannell, P., Schlesinger, P. and Sparks, C. (1985). *Media, Culture & Society: A Critical Reader.* London: Sage.

Curran, J. and Gurevitch, M. (eds) (1991). *Mass Communication and Society.* London: Edward Arnold.

Downing, J., Mohammadi, A. and Sreberny-Mohammadi, A. (eds) (1995). *Questioning the Media: A Critical Introduction.* 2nd edn. London: Sage.

During, S. (ed.) (1993). *The Cultural Studies Reader.* London: Routledge.

Hill, J. and Church Gibson, P. (eds) (1998). *The Oxford Guide to Film Studies.* Oxford: Oxford University Press.

Mattelart, A. and Siegelaub, S. (eds) (1979, 1983). *Communication and Class Struggle: An Anthology,* 2 vols. New York: International General Editions.

Moragas M. de (ed.) (1985). *Sociología de la communicación de masas,* 4 vols. Barcelona: Gustavo Gili.

The Polity Reader in Cultural Theory (1993). Cambridge: Polity Press.

Scannell, P., Schlesinger, P. and Sparks, C. (1992). *Culture and Power: A Media, Culture & Society Reader.* London: Sage.

Selected journals

Asian Journal of Communication (Singapore).

Communication (Québec).

Communication Research Trends (St Louis).

Communication Theory (Austin and New York).

Communications (Paris).

Critical Studies in Mass Communication. Dia-Logos (Lima), publication connected with the 'Red iberoamericana de revistas de comunicación y cultura' (Iberoamerican network of some 15 journals of communication and culture).

Hermès (Paris).

Journal of Communication (Philadelphia).

Journal of European Communication (London).

Journal of International Communication (Sydney).

Media, Culture & Society (London).

Nordicom Review (Göteborg).

Public Opinion Quarterly (Chicago).

Réseaux (Paris).

Réseaux: French Journal of Communication (London).

Telos (Madrid).

Index

LaVergne, TN USA
03 November 2009
162825LV00001B/5/A

9 780761 956471